Race Talk in a Mexican Cantina

Race Talk in a Mexican Cantina

Tatcho Mindiola

Michigan State University Press • *East Lansing*

Michigan State University Press
East Lansing, Michigan 48823-5245

Library of Congress Cataloging-in-Publication Data
Names: Mindiola, Tatcho, author.
Title: Race talk in a Mexican cantina / Tatcho Mindiola.
Description: East Lansing : Michigan State University Press, [2021] |
Series: Latinos in the United States | Includes bibliographical references and index.
Identifiers: LCCN 2020049157 | ISBN 978-1-61186-399-4 (paperback)
| ISBN 978-1-60917-673-0 | ISBN 978-1-62895-441-8 | ISBN 978-1-62896-435-6
Subjects: LCSH: Houston (Tex.)—Race relations. | Mexican Americans—Texas—Houston—Attitudes.
| Whites—Texas—Houston—Attitudes. | Working class men—Texas—Houston—Attitudes.
| Racism in language. | Racism—United States—Psychological aspects—Case studies.
| Benavides' Drive Inn (Bar : Houston, Tex.) | Bars (Drinking establishments)—
Social aspects—Texas—Houston. | Social interaction—United States—Case studies.
Classification: LCC F394.H89 A255 2021 | DDC 305.8009764/1411—dc23
LC record available at https://lccn.loc.gov/2020049157

Book and cover design by Charlie Sharp, Sharp Des|gns, East Lansing, MI
Cover image: Photo of JB's bar by Tatcho Mindiola.

Michigan State University Press is a member of the Green Press Initiative and is
committed to developing and encouraging ecologically responsible publishing
practices. For more information about the Green Press Initiative and the use of
recycled paper in book publishing, please visit *www.greenpressinitiative.org*.

Visit Michigan State University Press at *www.msupress.org*

Contents

Foreword

Rubén O. Martinez

orders circumscribe our lives across a broad range of dimensions. Mexican American and other Hispanics are located at cultural borders, most traversing them every day of their lives. In the Southwest, the mythical homeland of the Aztecs, where the majority of Mexican Americans reside, cultural border crossings are commonplace, but mostly on the part of the Spanish-speaking, who as an ethno-minority population must enter and contend with the culture of the dominant group. It is also where intergroup relations at the level of everyday life are constituted by interactions between Mexican Americans and white Americans. This book captures a critical aspect of those interactions by focusing on "race talk" among "Mexicans" and "whites" at a small Mexican bar in Houston, Texas.

These interactions took place in a setting that is key in situating their context: a working-class bar in Texas where the label "Mexican" is preferred by Mexican Americans. Every state in the Union has its own unique history, and Texas is no exception. It is a place with more than 180 years of relations between Mexicans and white Americans. It is also where Texan (white Texan) and Tejano (Mexican Texan) identities emerged. These are borderland identities grounded in conflictive and peaceful relations over time. They reflect a distinctive regional culture different from those of the rest of the country and manifest to varying degrees the borderlands culture of South Texas.

Houston was founded on the heels of the Texas Revolution by two real-estate brothers in 1836. They purchased the land on which the city was founded from the widow of John Austin, who had received a two-league grant of land from Stephen F. Austin, considered, from the white American perspective, the Father of Texas. Stephen had obtained an *empresario* (immigrant agent) contract with Mexico and claimed land his father Moses had obtained through a grant from the Spanish government. Moses had received a contract in 1820 to serve as *empresario* and entice settlers into the region, but died before fulfilling it. Mexico's independence, however, put ownership of some Spanish grants in question. In 1823, Stephen negotiated with Mexico's new leaders matters of land and received an *empresario* contract, much like that of his father, under Mexico's new colonization act. The area attracted Southern whites who brought with them preconceived notions of race and class. Decades later, during Reconstruction, Houston became a destination site for freed blacks.

Today, with nearly 2.33 million people, Houston is the fourth largest city in the United States and is home to one of the busiest ports. Over a million Latinos reside in Houston, constituting approximately 44 percent of the population. Mexican Americans make up approximately 80 percent of the Latino population. The Houston metro area, which extends into several counties, has approximately 7 million people, with about 38 percent Latinos. It is located within Harris County, which holds the second largest Latino population in the country. Los Angeles County has the largest. Houston also has sizable populations of African Americans, Asian Americans, and Asian immigrants. Additionally, Houston is projected to become a Latino majority city by 2050.

Houston's Second Ward is one of the original four wards. Its population was initially mostly German, becoming more diverse over time. Following World War II, Mexican Americans began moving in and today make up the majority of its population. Located in Houston's East End, which also has a majority Mexican American population, the ward is known as Segundo Barrio. Its northern end is mostly industrial, with large warehouse complexes along Buffalo Bayou. Considered a rundown area of the city, Second Ward is today in the early phases of gentrification.

It is here, in Segundo Barrio, where JB's bar was located, and where customers, mostly Mexicans and some whites, gathered to quaff a few beers and enjoy the camaraderie of others. It was a neighborhood bar where the customers knew each other and enjoyed each other's company. The bar was home to verbal sparring imbued with racial features between the Mexican and white customers, but also within members of the same group. Verbal sparring occurred in the presence of others, thereby taking on performative dimensions with group dynamics, much like the dozens game is played among African Americans. Among Mexicans, such verbal sparring is called *carrilla*, a form of teasing that usually involves a putdown. It can involve humor, metaphor, joke telling, wittiness, and cleverness. As in joke telling, timing is critical for achieving maximum impact.

What is unique about this book is its focus on what the author, Tatcho Mindiola, calls "race talk." That is, the ways by which the customers, members of different ethnic groups, acknowledged the existence of racism and used it as a feature in their verbal sparring. Rather than ignore racism as a feature of American society, the customers sometimes focused on racial roles, racial hierarchy, and racial stereotypes to poke fun at each other, sometimes eliciting hostile responses. There are many dimensions to their performances, including affiliative humor, which is more common among the working class than among middle and upper classes, which are more likely to be characterized by aggressive humor. Readers will enjoy learning about the different personalities and their favorite ways of engaging in playful yet cutting sparring sessions as they maintained interpersonal relationships.

Perhaps the open acknowledgment of racism by members of dominant and subordinate groups is in a sense taboo when in public spaces. The customers at JB's, however, played with it in their interpersonal relationships. Mindiola has taken an aspect of intergroup relations as they occurred in a Mexican-majority neighborhood bar between Mexicans and whites and presents it here for all of us to read. It is my hope that more scholarly works will examine "race talk" in different settings and between different groups and show the many ways by which people negotiate racial identities in public spaces, and how those identities and attendant racial roles are changing in the United States, hopefully for the better.

Acknowledgments

The following colleagues read and commented on parts or all of the manuscript. In alphabetical order their assistance is graciously acknowledged. Professor Gil Cardenas, Notre Dame University; Professor Teresa Córdova, University of Illinois at Chicago; Associate Professor Elizabeth Farfan Santos, University of Houston; Professor Joe Feagin, Texas A&M University; Professor Juan Gomez Quinones, University of California, Los Angeles; Professor Jose Limon, University of Texas, Austin; Professor David Montejano, University of California, Berkeley; Professor Nestor Rodriguez, University of Texas, Austin; Professor Guadalupe San Miguel, University of Houston; Professor Robert Trevino, University of Texas, Arlington. The following University of Houston students assisted with the research: Lilian Chavez and Felipe Vargas transcribed interviews, Oscar Oviedo and Jimmy Patino—now Associate Professor, University of Minnesota—organized the field notes. A special acknowledgment for Professor Rubén Martinez, Director of the Julian Samora Research Institute at Michigan State University, for his encouragement, and suggestions, and for my wife Cindy, who patiently read the manuscript and likewise made suggestions.

Introduction

This book analyzes the race talk that occurred among the men who patronized JB's Drive Inn, a small Mexican cantina located in Second Ward in Houston's East End, the oldest Mexican barrio in the city (De Leon 2001). I refer to JB's as a Mexican bar, but it was not an immigrant bar. The U.S.-born Mexicans who patronized the bar referred to themselves as Mexicans and hence my use of the term. The patrons used other self-referent labels, but Mexican and the slang term "Meskin" were their terms of choice, with Mexican being foremost. The official name of the bar was Benavides' Drive Inn, but everyone called it JB's after its owner, Jesse Benavides Jr. JB's Drive Inn was what Cavan (1966) called a "home territory bar." These bars were in distinct areas of cities and patronized by a group of people who shared a common social identity and perceived the bar as their social center. This described JB's. Most of the regular patrons were U.S.-born middle-aged Mexican males who had been friends for many years, some since childhood. A small group of middle-aged white men were also among the long-standing patrons. Most of JB's patrons were blue-collar workers, but there were a noticeable number of middle-class patrons as well.

This ethnography differs from other ethnographies on taverns in several respects. *Blue Collar Aristocrats* (LeMasters 1975) for example describes the Oasis tavern, whose patrons were white skilled laborers. By comparison, it is a relatively mild book. Indeed, the author states that he deliberately did not record the patrons' profanity because he did not think they would want it recorded and made public. In addition, the race talk was limited. The white patrons were opposed to integration, did not believe that blacks were equal to whites in intelligence, and were adamantly opposed to mixed racial couples. Militant African American activists such as Rap Brown and Stokely Carmichael raised their ire. Another ethnography that dealt with a drinking establishment is *The World from Brown's Lounge* (Bell 1983). Middle-class African Americans patronized this bar. The author was a white male college student studying English, but surprisingly the patrons did not say anything about his race. Apparently, it was not an issue beyond one patron telling him in private that he loved and hated him at the same time because he was white. The author did not respond to the patron. *Talking at Trena's* (May 2001) is also about an African American tavern. In two of the book's chapters, the author, an African American, describes how its patrons talked about their experiences with the police, how whites perceived them as intellectually inferior, and their physical conflicts with whites. They also discussed conspiracy theories: for example, the belief that O. J. Simpson, the former football star, did not murder his white wife and her white friend, but rather it was the Mafia. Trena's patrons also discussed television news about African Americans, and especially programs that featured African Americans and talk shows that dealt with mixed white-African American relations between males and females.

Two other books that dealt with race talk were also consulted: *Two Faced Racism* (Houts Picca and Feagin 2007) and *Race Talk* (Myers 2005). The race talk in both books, however, did not occur in a bar. The first documented how white college students talked about race in public and in private. In public, or the front stage, the white college students avoided making racist or any negative comments about other races. In private all-white settings, or the backstage, however, negative racial sentiments abounded. The second book discusses how students and administrators in private all-white settings talked negatively about people who were not white, but avoided making such comments in public. Ethnographies dealing with Mexican cantinas do not exist, even though cantinas are present in cities where Mexicans reside. Thus, this ethnography about the ongoing race talk between the Mexican and white patrons is the first of its kind and will make a contribution to the study of drinking establishments and interactions between Mexicans and whites by beginning to fill in a void in the literature.

My introduction to JB's came about one evening in 2003 when a colleague and I stopped in the bar to have a beer and talk. We selected JB's for no other reason than it was on our way home. I had often seen the bar as I drove through Second Ward, but until that evening, I had never visited or known anything about it. The bar was small and dimly lit. The only light was from the neon beer signs that gave the dimness a blue hue. There were four men inside the bar, three patrons and the bartender, who was behind the bar. One of the patrons was standing in between the other two, who were sitting on bar stools. He was dominating the conversation with stories about his adventures as an undercover police officer. The bartender and two patrons were listening intently. We heard bits and pieces of the man's story, the persons he arrested and how and why and what he told them. He was an animated performer with an attentive audience. My colleague and I left after about an hour, and on our way home I mentioned that the patrons' stories were a good example of macho talk. He agreed and that was the extent of our conversation about the bar. I cannot explain why, but the imagery of the bar, its small size, the bluish hue, the macho talk, remained with me in the days that followed, and I began thinking about going back for the explicit purpose of seeing what I could find out. Perhaps, I thought, there was an interesting story to be found. I spoke with my colleague and invited him to join me in my exploration, but he was involved with other research projects and was hesitant to commit. I nevertheless decided to visit the bar again.

Race Talk

My second visit occurred three weeks later, on a rainy Friday afternoon around 3 p.m. I stood at one end of the bar and took in the scene. The place was smaller than I thought, and I saw a sign over the door that read "Official Capacity, 25 people." I counted seventeen patrons: twelve Mexicans and five whites. It was crowded. The atmosphere was festive, with talk and laughter seemingly hanging in the air. Everyone seemed to know everyone else. Two things quickly caught my attention: the profanity and the race talk. The profanity was abundant. No one, it seemed, could utter a sentence without using profane language. Their comments were punctuated with "fuck you," "son of a bitch," and "motherfucker." In a couple of instances, the profanity dominated a sentence, as in "I told that motherfucker 'you can't do shit' you son of a bitch." One grandfatherly looking Mexican patron surprised me when he uttered a string of expletives. His kindly appearance was incongruous with his excessive profanity. The phone rang. One of the patrons answered. "You son of a bitch, where are you?" he yelled into the phone. "I bet that's JB," someone said. The Canal Street door swung open with force and a Mexican man walked in holding his cell phone to his ear. "I'm right here you s-o-b," he said loudly, "and I'm going to kick your ass." Everyone laughed as he walked through the bar shaking hands and exchanging comments. It was indeed JB.

The race talk began when two of the white patrons left. At the time, I did not know the patrons' names, but learned them later and have inserted them in my notes.

> The heavy-set white man (Jerry) standing next to me looks around and says out loud to no one in particular, "Well, there are only three whites in here now, there were five." The tall white man (White Mike) sitting at one of the tables responds, "That's okay, we can still handle them." His comment receives laughter, jeers, and profanity from several of the Mexicans. "Fuck you," "you wish," "bring it on," they respond. Everyone is laughing. The tall white patron at the other end of the bar (Manuel) has a huge grin on his face and is enjoying the give-and-take. One of the Mexican patrons

(Kid) opens the Canal Street door and watches it rain. "Damn," he says, "it's a good day to hang a white man." Everyone laughs. "Hey," the white patron (White Mike) at the table calls out to the Mexican patron (Leo) playing the 8 Liner slot machine, "he's using your line." "Shit," the Mexican patron responds as he takes a drink of his beer, "any day is a good day to hang a white man." Everyone laughs again, but this time it is louder and there is hooting. Again, I notice how much the white patron at the other end of the bar (Manuel) is laughing and enjoying the give-and-take.

The exchange was intriguing. Research reports that in mixed racial settings, whites avoid speaking about race from fear of saying something wrong (Houts Picca and Feagin 2007; Bonilla-Silva 2006; Myers 2005), but this was not what I observed and heard in the bar. My interest was piqued. Over the weeks that followed, I visited the bar several more times to assess if the race talk could have been an anomaly. It was not. The racial exchanges were an integral, ongoing part of the Mexican-white relationship in the bar. They were not the primary topic, but they were consistent and noticeable. Thus, I made a decision to conduct an ethnographic study with the intent of observing, recording, and analyzing the race talk between the Mexican and white patrons. After speaking with JB and receiving his approval, and meeting university requirements, I began visiting the bar on a regular basis and recording my observations. Over a three-year period from 2003 to 2006, I made more than five hundred visits, spent an average of two to three hours per visit, and recorded 490 entries about what I observed and heard. Early into the research I attempted to set up taped interviews with the patrons to delve into the topics discussed in the following chapters, but to no avail. Some of the patrons told me directly that they did not do interviews, and others told me they would think about it, while others laughed and said they did not have anything to say. A few told me they would do an interview but then would put me off when I tried to set a date and time. Thus, I gave up the effort to do interviews and rather asked questions when appropriate during my visits.

Although the focus was upon the race talk, I recorded everything that I heard immediately upon leaving the bar. If circumstances did not allow for a quick recording, I made brief outlines and recorded my observations as soon as time allowed, usually later that evening or the following morning, but more than 95 percent of the entries were made immediately after I left the bar. My notes consisted of three thousand typed pages, and the quotes that are presented in this study are taken from my notes.

Conducting Research in Your Backyard

Approximately three weeks into my visits, I realized that very few strangers ever patronized JB's. It was always the same people and mostly men. Whenever I saw people whom I had not seen before, they usually turned out to be former patrons. Occasionally strangers ventured into the bar, but they never stayed long and rarely, if ever, returned. Only three new patrons joined the group of regulars during the study and I was one of them. The other two were white patrons brought to the bar by White Mike, the pipe fitter, and this facilitated their acceptance and integration into the bar's dynamics. I did not have a sponsor, but neither was I a stranger, for I encountered people whom I knew. Geraldo, the attorney, was an example. I have known Geraldo and his brothers on a casual basis for many years. He greeted me the first time he saw me, and over time I learned that he was a close friend of JB and had been a regular patron ever since the bar opened. I also encountered Rubio and Gene, two Mexican patrons who had been golfing buddies with my two oldest, now deceased, brothers, Gilbert and Mondo. Rubio and Gene had likewise been patrons since the bar opened and were lifelong friends with JB. At the time of the study, both were retired. Other patrons had seen me on television commenting about politics, education, immigration, and related issues. Some were university alumni, a few were former students, and at least on three occasions I encountered the husbands of former students. These patrons were semi-regular customers, but they always expressed surprise when they saw me, and all posed similar responses such as "What are you doing here?" One of my more interesting encounters was with Manuel, one of the white patrons. Manuel lived in the same neighborhood where I grew up, in the Sunset Heights located on the north side of Houston. He was friends with my oldest brother, Mondo, and there was a time in their lives when they knew each other well. I did not recognize Manuel when I first saw him, but one afternoon when I heard JB call out his full name I immediately knew who he was and at the appropriate time introduced myself. He did not remember me, but he recalled that Mondo had several brothers, and his first question was "Which brother are you?" We spent the next hour or so talking about our families and people we both knew from years past. Over time he began telling the other patrons that he had known me most of his life. At the time of the study Manuel was retired after being a long-distance truck driver for most of his adult life. He also had been the owner of a bar located in Houston's Northside that had a predominantly Mexican clientele.

Another discovery had even more personal ramifications and concerned JB. Three months into my visits I discovered that JB and I were distant cousins. His grandfather was the brother of my wife's grandfather on her mother's side. This meant that JB's father and my wife's deceased mother were first cousins and that JB and my wife were second cousins. It also meant that JB and I were second cousins through marriage. After we discovered this, JB and I started calling each other "cousin" or "cuz" and it became known in the bar that we were kin. I also met Troy, whose father was the brother of one of my uncles. This meant that Troy's father was also my uncle. We likewise started calling each other "cuz." Troy worked in maintenance for the local gas company. A few of the patrons also were friends with Paul, a first cousin, who lived in the Denver Harbor barrio. These factors facilitated my acceptance and integration into the bar's regular group of patrons.

Part of my research strategy was to deflect my status as a professor as much as possible. Educated people, especially those with PhDs, are often viewed as thinking, acting, and believing they are intellectually superior, and I did not want to convey this impression. For the most part, I avoided discussions about the university, but it was impossible to shed the professorial status. Most of the time the patrons addressed me as Professor, as in "How you are doing Professor?" or "Want a beer Professor?" or "How have you been Professor?" A few patrons referred to me as the in-house professor or the resident professor, and once when I approached a group on the deck on the side of the bar, Adolph, one of the Mexican patrons, said, "The Professor is here, now we have to talk intelligently." Sometimes the patrons would address me by my first name. Efren, a retired teamster, called me Mr. Tatcho, and Mr. Charlie, the Mexican octogenarian and retired salesclerk, called me Tatchito, but mostly I was called Professor. The patrons also saw me as an expert and asked questions about history, immigration, politics, race, gun laws, finance, the war in Iraq, and other issues. My professorship was also a target for teasing. One evening, after I had won my second domino game in a row, Leo, the president of the local teamster union, said, "The Nutty Professor wins again." Everyone laughed and for a while I heard the term frequently. Once after I was called the Nutty Professor a patron laughed and said, "I like that, it fits." I never deciphered exactly what he meant.

Working in the Bar

I usually visited the bar in the afternoons when most of the white patrons were more likely to be present and the race talk was more apt to occur. These visits generated comments about my work schedule. Gilbert, a used-car salesman and one of the Mexican patrons, was especially vocal. He repeatedly asked, "Are you off work already?" or "Are you going back to work?" At times, he expressed exasperated disbelief. "Damn, Professor, are you already off work?" he asked, or he would say, "Damn! You never work." I usually smiled and ignored his comments, but on one occasion, I responded by saying, "I am working," to which he said, "Well, you have a great job because you are always here." Others made similar comments. White Mike, one of the white patrons and a pipe fitter, once asked how I was feeling, and when I replied, "underpaid," he retorted with "Well hell, I can see why, you're always here." On another afternoon, when I walked into the bar, Paul, another white patron and pipe fitter, remarked, "Damn Professor, don't you ever work?" It was also believed that I was naive about the rough-and-tumble world of men like those at JB's because of my professorship. These notions stemmed from a stereotype that professors lived in an ivory tower of abstract knowledge and therefore were divorced from the real world. When the profanity was especially excessive, the patrons would comment, "The Professor is not used to it being so rough" or "The Professor is not used to hearing this kind of talk." Mr. Charlie often apologized. "I'm sorry you're hearing that kind of talk," he would tell me. "I don't speak that way and I'm not used to hearing that type of language." This always brought forth accusations that he was the most prolific purveyor of such talk.

Drinking is one of the reasons for patronizing a bar, but it is not the primary reason. Conversation—that is, interaction—is the primary reason, but it works in tandem with and facilitated by drinking (Oldenburg 1989). I tempered my drinking to meet the purpose of the research, and I accomplished this by simply monitoring how much I drank or not drinking at all. Many times, I purchased a bucket of beer and shared it with the others. This made it easier to drink one beer slowly for a long period of time without being noticed. About halfway through the research, I realized that a noticeable sum of money had gone into purchasing buckets and treating other patrons. Consequently, I wrote the Internal Revenue Service (IRS) asking if I could deduct the cost as a research expense. It facilitated my acceptance in the bar and was crucial to meeting the research objective, I stated. The IRS responded with a one-sentence letter of denial stating that it was not an essential expense or condition for the research. It was essential, however, given that drinking was a main norm and one of the ways one became part of the group. It was noticed when I refused a beer, and I offered a variety of excuses. I said I had to return to work, had eaten a late lunch and felt too full to drink, or had a function to attend later in the evening. All these excuses carried a degree of truth, but the real reason was being attentive to the conversations.

The Lenten season also provided an excuse as I stopped consuming alcohol. During Lent, JB was gracious enough to purchase a nonalcoholic beer for me. I did not know when he ordered it that it came in a green bottle and as a result became a source of teasing because it stood out in comparison to the brown bottled beer that JB sold. It reminded patrons of my abstinence. They referred to the beer as "the green ones" and asked why I was drinking it. The most common reaction, however, was some of the patrons telling me about their Lenten sacrifices, past and present. Several said they used to give up "something for Lent" and often the item sacrificed was alcohol. When Leo learned that the green ones were nonalcoholic and the reasons why I drank it, he called me a "religious freak" and "our parishioner." Geraldo, the attorney, said that I was "trying to be good" and "drinking religious water" so I could "get into heaven." Others who were not Catholic asked, "What's the point?" Each year I extended my drinking of the green ones beyond Lent to finish whatever quantity JB had purchased, and this, likewise, generated comment. Gilbert would ask, "You still drinking that green shit?" or he would say, "I thought Lent was over," and on a couple of occasions when I ordered a green one he told me, "Hell man, drink a real beer." When I finished the green ones and again drank regular beer, patrons took note. Comments included "glad you're back," "do you feel better?" and "it feels better to be normal and drink, doesn't it?" Leo asked, "Are you free again?" and when Gilbert saw me again drinking regular beer he said, "It's about time."

Social Space of Play

Drinking establishments like JB's Drive Inn are social spaces of play where people go to drink, relax, and seek enjoyment through interaction with others. Playtime is different from "real" or "ordinary" time, which is task oriented and filled with things people must do—for example, work. Playtime in contrast is voluntary. It is a choice invoked. If play is compelled it ceases to be play because the freedom to choose has been taken away (Huizinga 1949). People are especially apt to say and do things in social spaces of play because the conventional norms of behavior are relaxed, and people feel free to be who they really are or seek to be. Playtime reduces stress and alienation, gives relief from authority, and fosters bonding among friends. This was especially true in JB's, where the consumption of alcohol, primarily beer, acted as a relaxer and lessened inhibitions, as illustrated by the profanity, teasing, and laughter. Profanity and teasing are aggressive acts, and laughter is a feel-good emotion that releases the tensions that profanity or teasing can induce. In JB's, all three were intertwined. Laughter is particularly indicative of bars as social spaces of play because drinkers laugh more in comparison to nondrinkers (Lowe and Taylor 1997, 1993), and laughter was abundant in JB's. More than 2,300 instances of laughter were recorded during the three years the study was conducted. Serious conversations did occur, but gaiety was the norm.

Machismo

JB's was also a social space of play for males who tend to be more aggressive when performing in front of other males. Men seek affirmation of their manhood from both males and females, but validation from other males is more important to their notions of masculinity. Men strive to be a man among men, and this leads to displays of aggression, dominance, bravado, and toughness, the characteristics of hypermasculinity (Kimmel 2017). In the English-speaking world, the Spanish word *macho* describes hypermasculinity. This reinforces a stereotype that Mexicans and other males whose origins are rooted in Spain are more prone to machismo in comparison to other males. This, of course, is not true. Hypermasculinity is a worldwide phenomenon and exists in every culture on earth (Gilmore 1990). In the United States, hypermasculinity among the Mexican and white males is described in the same manner, usually negative, and includes behaviors of dominance, a belief that risk-taking and danger are exciting, that violence is manly, and that males are superior to women (Paredes 2003; Mosher 1991; Mirande 1986; Money 1980). Positive depictions of machismo present a man of honor, respect, dignity, strength, and the head of the household and protector of the family (Mirande 1997). Both the positive and negative aspects of machismo were observed among JB's patrons, but the term that best described their displays of machismo was aggression, the forceful and assertive ways in which the patrons interacted with each other. Their interactions were laden with profanity, teasing, and posturing. These displays of aggressive machismo, however, were variable, with some of JB's patrons exhibiting more macho behavior than others did. Some patrons like the pipe fitter Anthony, a Mexican patron, rarely exhibited macho behavior. He was the bar's least assuming patron and inclined to listen rather than talk, and when he did speak, he did so in a soft voice, yet he was a blue-collar worker with a manly appearance. His overall demeanor, however, was relatively less aggressive. Other patrons emphasized certain aspects of machismo such as the Ladies' Man (Glass 1984). They bragged about their conquests and flirted in a very affectionate and sexual manner with the few women who patronized the bar. The majority of the patrons, however, displayed the full range of macho behavior with varying degrees of intensity depending upon the circumstances and topics.

Race as a Social Construction

The focus is upon the race talk between the Mexican and white patrons and what they said about each other's race and African Americans. This raised the issue of the validity of race as a biological and genetic concept. According to Smedley and Smedley (2005), between the sixteenth and eighteenth centuries the term *race* was a folk idea interchangeable with other terms such as *type, kind, sort, breed,* and *species*. By the end of the Revolutionary era in 1783, the term race had solidified to refer to immutable differences between whites and nonwhites, specifically indigenous Indians and African Americans, who were described as the inferior races. Whites used this alleged inferiority to justify taking lands from the indigenous Indians and enslaving African Americans. The inferiority thesis was also used when white Americans went to war with Mexico to take the Texas territory away in 1836 and the greater southwestern part of the United States in 1848.

Two and a half centuries later, biological and genetics research shows that there are no significant differences between the races (Guo et al. 2014). Indeed, the research has established that there is less than 0.01 difference in biology and genetics between the white and darker-skinned races and race is now understood as a social construction (Smedley and Smedley 2005). Yet, most Americans continue to accept that there are significant and immutable genetic and biological differences between the various races, with whites viewed as the superior race. The law further reinforced race as immutable category (Martinez 1997). The U.S. Census and social-science surveys also ask people to identify their race under the assumption that it helps explain their behavior (Guo et al. 2014; Townsley 2007). People in general believe that racial differences are real, and if people believe that something is real, they are real in their consequences (Thomas 1929). In the United States, for example, there is a racial stratification system with whites on top, followed by Mexicans and then African Americans. Mexicans are closer to African Americans in economic status but are closer in social prestige to whites because of their greater variety in skin color. Mexicans who have a light complexion are more acceptable to whites than the darker-skinned Mexicans, but Mexicans in general, like African Americans, are still not seen as equal to whites as human beings.

The analysis of the race talk between the Mexican and white patrons presented in this study are an example of how racial differences as a social reality were continuously being reproduced through interaction. Most studies of race talk tend to analyze how groups of racially homogeneous people talk about race among themselves. Studies of race talk in mixed racial settings are rare. One African American scholar, for example, writes that he had a white friend in college who was one of his best friends (Yancey 2007). They were always together, visited each other's homes, coached intramural sports, and attended social events. They talked about everything under the sun: girls, sports, their areas of study, their futures, politics, and religion—everything, that is, except race. Why? He did not think his white friend could relate to racism, so he never brought it up. Two studies of interracial friendships did address the issue of race. One analyzed forty interracial friendships involving blacks and whites and reported they handled race in one of three ways. It was avoided, seriously discussed, or joked about (Korgen 2002). The content of the discussions and jokes and the effect upon their relationships, however, were not described. The second study described how court-mandated school integration in the rural south in the 1960s brought white teachers to black schools for the first time ever (Peterson 1975). The teachers encountered resistance and resentment, especially from the students, and to make matters worse, they did not know anything about African American culture and what they did know was stereotypical. Over time, a young white male teacher turned to his black male colleagues for advice on how to deal with difficult students. The black teachers had taken notice of his sincere efforts to work with the students, and when approached, they teased him about his inexperience and his white background while giving him advice. He accepted their teasing and over time began joking about his problems, while receiving their advice as to how to improve his classroom practices. The black teachers eventually began joking with the white female teachers as well, but only after they had established formal working relationships. What was relevant about the research for this study was the role that humor played in releasing racial tensions. It pulled the two groups together through their sharing of levity. It relaxed them and made them aware of their commonalities, but Peterson did not describe the content of the joking. Given that race talk was the focus of this research, it may create an impression that it was a primary preoccupation of JB's patrons, but this would be an erroneous assumption. It was an integral part of the Mexican-white relationship, and while it may not have been the primary concern, it was nevertheless a consistent topic that revealed that their racial consciousness was never far away from activation. As a topic, it ranked third behind family and drinking.

Humor

Most of the race talk between the Mexican and white patrons occurred within the context of humor, specifically joking and teasing. It was dialogical game of one-upmanship, with the Mexicans winning the contest because they were the majority group and whites the minority group. The humorous context signaled that the racial comments were not serious but said in jest and everyone was "just kidding." This helped inoculate the speaker against any negative reaction (Skalicky, Berger, and Bell 2015). Yet, the teasing and joking contained messages. Someone was going to be the butt of ridicule and laughter because of his race. The race talk therefore had the potential to anger and cause resentment on the part of those who were the butt of the jokes, and when this happened, the hidden racial antagonisms became apparent. Furthermore, the race talk did not occur in a social vacuum. It reflected circumstances informed by the historical and contemporary events that influenced Mexican-white relations in the United States. Consider the scene described earlier. Jerry, a white patron, indicated that he was feeling "like a minority" by expressing an awareness of being vastly outnumbered by the Mexican patrons. This feeling of otherness, however, did not bother White Mike. He was a white man in a Mexican bar, in the Mexican side of town, with only a handful of white patrons present, and yet he proclaimed, "We can still handle them." This display of macho bravado was reminiscent of the Texas Ranger who was sent to quell a Mexican riot. When he arrived, legend has it, he was asked why only one Ranger was sent, to which he replied, "There's only one riot isn't there?" (Jackson and Wilkinson 2005). This was White Mike's implied message: regardless of the odds, it does not take many whites to handle a bunch of Mexicans because whites are superior to Mexicans. The Mexican patrons, however, pushed back with their own aggressive comments and displays of machismo. They cursed White Mike, challenged his assertions, and the indiscriminate hanging of whites was said to be a good thing, the weather notwithstanding. In Texas, history informs us, the Mexicans were the hanging victims, but in the bar, whites were the potential hanging victims. Also, it was apparent this was not the first time that the Mexican sentiment of "any day is a good day to kill a white man" was expressed, as indicated by White Mike telling Leo, "He's using your line," alluding to the ongoing racial performances in the bar. The exchange, though humorous, contained a message that reflected the history of Mexican-white relations. In addition, the remarks by the patrons were instantaneous, automatic, with the whites' assertions of superiority being met with pushback, resistance, and the last word coming from the Mexican patrons, the dominant pattern in the bar.

Incongruence and Microaggressions

Whites have an inherent advantage in society over Mexicans. To grasp this situation is to have congruence, that is, to understand that whites have more power and prestige relative to Mexicans. In the bar the situation was reversed. JB's was Mexican turf and the Mexican patrons were the majority, with more power and prestige relative to whites, and they acted in like manner. The situation in the bar, in other words, was incongruent. The white patrons pushed back and criticized the Mexican patrons, but as will be shown, their criticisms were milder and less frequent in comparison to what they received. The attacks and criticism that both the Mexican and white patrons leveled at each other are best understood as microaggressions, which are defined as racial slights, indignities, putdowns, and insults (Delgado and Stefancic 2017; Sue 2010). They were deliberate and an integral part of the ongoing interactions between the Mexican and white patrons, and though uttered by both, the Mexicans had the upper hand in the frequency and content of the microaggressions. It was this situation that made the race talk in the bar unique, for the literature on microaggressions emphasizes that minorities are the victims and whites are the perpetrators (Sue 2010).

Thick Description and Impressionist Tales

The style in which this ethnography is presented was influenced by the ideas of Clifford Geertz (1973) and John Van Maanen (2011). These scholars emphasized describing people's interactions, their settings and circumstances, in detailed fashion to include the relationships among the actors—their emotions, motives, and the way they presented themselves. Geertz referred to this style of ethnographic presentation as "thick description" while Van Maanen labeled it as "impressionist tales." Their goal was to present as true a picture as possible of the social reality being described so that readers could more fully understand and empathize with the social reality under consideration. This emphasis led to a storytelling style of presenting information, but as indicated, it was also informed by the relevant research.

CHAPTER ONE

The Bar

JB's Drive Inn is located on the corner of Canal and Drennen in the heart of Second Ward, the oldest Mexican neighborhood in the city of Houston. Second Ward was established in 1837 by the Allen brothers, who divided the city into political districts known as wards a year after they founded Houston on the banks of Buffalo Bayou. Germans, Italians, and Irish residents initially inhabited Second Ward (Kreneck 2012; De Leon 1986). The three main streets crossing the barrio and running parallel to each other were named Harrisburg, Canal, and Navigation. Harrisburg commemorates the first capital of Texas, which was established near Houston, and Navigation and Canal Streets were so named because of Second Ward's proximity to the Port of Houston. Canal Street was initially named German Street, reflecting the influence of the German population in the area, but it was changed in 1918 because of the anti-German sentiment that emanated from World War I.

The Mexican Revolution of 1910 pushed Mexicans out of Mexico, and economic opportunity pulled them into Houston's Second Ward during the early 1900s. Many also migrated from South Texas. They were primarily of the lower classes, but some middle- and upper-class people came as well. Most moved to Second Ward because it was close to the railroad yards, manufacturing plants, and Port of Houston where work could be found. Public transportation was not available in the area and people could walk to work. As the Mexicans kept moving into the area, the white population began to leave. Mexicans also began moving into the adjacent area of Magnolia Park because it was closer to the Port. By the 1930s a large Mexican community had established itself in the area, and it is in Second Ward and Magnolia Park that one finds the first Mexican church, mutualista organizations, funeral home, newspaper, radio station, parade, sports teams, civic organizations, and commercial districts that stretched into the northern part of downtown Houston.

Today approximately 16,000 people live in the Second Ward barrio and the population is 74 percent Hispanic, 13 percent white, and 13 percent African American (Community Health Profile 2003). Approximately one-third of the Mexican population is immigrant and the remaining two-thirds are second- and third-generation U.S.-born Mexicans. It is still a relatively poor community with all the attendant ills, but a stable blue-collar population and smaller middle class are found among the residents. Within the last two decades, whites have been patronizing the Mexican restaurants and the markets in the northern part of Second Ward, and it has become a tourist area. Developers have also purchased old homes and warehouses in the area and have begun replacing them with condominiums, which is drawing a younger, white professional social class who likewise patronize the various local business establishments.

JB's grandparents moved into Second Ward in 1926 when his mother was five years old. They were among the area's first Mexican residents. JB's father and mother met in Second Ward, married, and lived all their lives a few blocks away from where the bar would be eventually established. JB was born in 1947 and has four brothers and four sisters. JB said his father was "a hustler" and always worked two or three jobs while his mother remained at home tending to the family. JB went to elementary and junior high in the area but only attended high school "part time" and was asked to leave because of poor attendance. He then attended a technical and vocational school but left the program and joined the Marines. Upon discharge at the age of twenty-one, JB returned to Second Ward and worked at several of the manufacturing plants in the area. In 1975, he began working for his father, who was leasing a gas station next to the property where he would eventually open a bar.

JB said the idea of a bar occurred to him while working at the service station. During the gas shortage crisis of the 1970s, gas sales went down and JB and his brother Richard, aka Kid, started selling beer out of the service station to make up for the lost revenue. JB put beer cans in the Coca-Cola machine and sold it to the patrons who stopped for gas or service. He quickly noticed they sold a lot of beer. According to JB, "If it wasn't for the beer, I don't know how we would have made it. Man, everybody in Second Ward would buy beer from us." The lucrative beer sales motivated JB to purchase the vacant building next door and establish a bar. According to the City of Houston Directory, the building that became the bar was built in 1956 (*Kriss Kross Directory*). For most of its history, the building was occupied by auto repair shops. When JB purchased the building in 1978, it had been vacant for ten years. He converted it into a drinking establishment, named it Benavides' Drive Inn, and opened in 1980. "I started selling beer for a living full time while Richard continued to run the service station," he told me. In between the service station and the bar was a vacant lot where JB placed picnic tables. Patrons bought beer at the bar, sat at the tables, and drank and talked while their cars were being attended to at the service station.

The small bar sits on 10,000 square feet of land and this provided ample parking space for the patrons. In 1992, JB added a 170-square-foot deck on one side of the bar. During special events, there could be upwards of one hundred people in attendance filling the bar, deck, and its surrounding area. In the front of the bar and to the right was a mobile taqueria. JB rented this space to the taqueria owner, but JB's patrons were not his customers. Across the street were two dance halls that catered to Salvadorians and other Central Americans and they were the taqueria's primary customers, especially after the dance halls closed late at night. On the Drennen Street side of the bar was a large manufacturing firm owned by an African American. On the other side was the service station that JB and Kid had operated with their father. Now it was a mechanic shop that was operated by men from Mexico.

The inside of the bar was small. It occupied 432 square feet including the restrooms. There were two entrances, one on Drennan Street and the other on Canal Avenue. The Drennan entrance was the official address, but everyone used the entrance on Canal Avenue as the main entry. On balance, the bar was nondescript, but its small size made for an intimate atmosphere. It was easy to move around and interact with everyone. Often everyone was focused on the same conversation or on the domino game. The bar's small size magnified the personalities that gave the bar its color and flair because everyone was physically close to each other.

The Mexican Patrons

Neighborhood bars have always serviced an ethnic, social-class, or other type of demographic from the geographical area where they are located. Neighborhood bars have usually been havens for males (Oldenburg 1989), and thus it was with JB's. The bar serviced a predominately blue-collar, working-class Mexican male clientele from the immediate and surrounding area. Ninety percent of JB's patrons were Mexicans. An estimated 45 percent grew up in Second Ward and many still lived and worked in the area. If the adjacent barrio of Magnolia Park was included, approximately 70 percent of JB's Mexican patrons were raised, worked, and continued to live in or have a connection to the two barrios that made up a large area of Houston's inner-city East End. The Mexican patrons had been customers for an average of twenty-three years, but some had been visiting since the bar opened. Among the blue-collar workers were a skilled carpenter, energy-company lineman, butcher, pipe fitter, postal worker, warehouseman, manufacturing worker, and machinist. There were also several small business owners. One sold used cars, another owned a company that cleaned tanks at the Port of Houston, and another owned a company that printed logos on T-shirts, jackets, and caps. JB purchased T-shirts and caps from this patron with the name of the bar printed across the top of the caps in a color that contrasted with the cap's color. He ordered them at least once a year and gave them to the patrons. JB also purchased black jackets with "Benavides Drive Inn" printed in yellow on the back above a picture of his 1932 vintage Chevrolet. He sold the jackets to the patrons and printed their names in yellow on the front, high on the right side above the pocket. A few of the Mexican patrons were retired. Efren, for example, was a retired teamster and Mr. Charlie was a retired sales clerk. There were also a few middle-class professionals. They included a financial advisor, attorney, president of a Teamster's local union, accountant, bondsman, and a medical research technician. The attorney and bondsman owned their own businesses with offices in the area. Most of the middle-class patrons, however, did not live in the area, but they maintained an emotional connection as indicated by their regular patronage of the bar. They were examples of the adage that "you can take the boy out of the barrio, but you can't take the barrio out of the boy."

A group of police officers were also part of the Mexican patrons. Most were still active officers and two were retired. The majority were members of the Houston Police Department and two were county deputy constables. All but three of the officers grew up in the East End and were patrolling or had patrolled their old neighborhoods. They perceived JB's as a safe place for a police officer to drink because "everyone knows everyone, and we don't have to watch our backs." Only four Mexican females patronized the bar during the study, but in a semi-regular manner. One was a special-education teacher, another was a nurse, and two were unemployed. Other females visited on Friday evenings and when celebrations took place.

All the Mexican male patrons except one were born in the United States and were highly acculturated into white culture as indicated by their flawless English-language dominancy, patriotism, and relative lack of philosophical, romantic, or emotional ties to Mexico as the motherland. They retained important aspects of their Mexican heritage, such as the Spanish language, food, music, and norms, but these had been so influenced by white culture that the Mexican culture they exhibited was syncretic, a mix of Mexican and white culture with white culture having dominance as exhibited by English being the predominant language in the bar. Efren was the only patron born in Mexico, but he had been in the United States most of his adult life as a citizen. He spoke English with an accent, and his birthplace, Mexico, served as a source of teasing. He and other Mexican patrons called each other wetbacks, but Efren was asserted to be "the only true wetback" in the bar. Once when Efren called Mexico "that wetback country," several patrons responded with "look who's talking," and "what the hell are you?"

The White Patrons

JB said he always had a small white clientele. In the early years of the bar's existence, one of his regular white customers was "old man Jeffery," who was one of his golfing friends. He had since died. A group of white sheriff's deputies once patronized on a regular basis as did a small group of white judges and lawyers. The white middle-aged men who were regular patrons at the time of the study constituted approximately 10 percent of JB's regular patrons and had been customers on average for seventeen years. Several, like White Mike, Jerry, and Mr. Jim, lived in nearby Mexican neighborhoods. Jerry owned a small remodeling company and all his workers were Mexicans from the United States and Mexico. One of the regular white patrons, Manuel, had been married to a Mexican woman and once owned a popular Mexican bar on Houston's Northside. At the time of the study, he was married to a woman from Central America. Tina worked at an insurance agency and was the only white woman who patronized the bar on a regular basis. One of the deputies had brought her to the bar sixteen years before. She said she liked JB and the rest of the patrons and felt that it was a safe place to drink and enjoy herself. The white patrons' employment consisted of blue-collar and white-collar occupations. The blue-collar patrons were pipe fitters and the white-collar occupations included affiliations with the insurance industry. There was also a small-business owner, a retired business owner, and a retired railroad clerk. Some of the white patrons, like Manuel, Wiley, Harvey, and Jerry, had been more than moderately successful financially.

Most of JB's regular patrons consisted of two groups, depending on the time of their patronage. One group came in the mid-afternoon after JB opened at 1 p.m. Most of these patrons held jobs that did not require them to punch a clock and a few were retired. The second group came in the late afternoon when they got off from work. This group tended to be larger than the early afternoon group. Both groups included patrons of long standing. The people who patronized the bar in the evenings after 7 p.m. were a mixture of regular and semi-regular patrons, but their numbers, at the time of the study, were not very large. Friday nights were an exception when the bar was packed with the regular patrons, some with their wives. Friday nights were also when a racially mixed group patronized the bar. It included two Mexican males and two Mexican women, one accompanied by her white husband and the other accompanied by her African American boyfriend. They all worked in the front office of a nearby department store warehouse. I visited most often during the early and late afternoons when the white patrons were more apt to be present, given that my interest was the race talk.

The Neighborhood Club

Neighborhood bars have generally served as semi-private clubs for their male patrons (Powers 1998; Oldenburg 1989; Mass Observation 1987; Popham 1962, 1978; Macrory 1952) as was the situation with JB's. Clubs are associations of people with similar characteristics that have a common purpose. The common purpose of JB's patrons, as in most neighborhood bars, was to engage in communal drinking, conversation, and enjoyment. They displayed their wit and verbosity as they told stories, aggressively teased each other, and engaged in exaggerated posturing.

The patrons of neighborhood bars also tend to be middle-aged men, and this likewise described JB's Mexican and white patrons, with the majority being in their fifties and sixties. There were also a small number of patrons in their early forties. Most of the patrons were married, had families, owned their homes, drove late-model cars, trucks, and SUVs, and were economically stable. They had similar working-class backgrounds, especially the patrons that grew up in the East End. Some were high school dropouts, others were graduates, and a few had college degrees. The patrons had known each other for a relatively long time, some since childhood. When the same people gather regularly over a long period of time, they create their own culture (May 2000, 2001; Thomas 1978; Room 1972). In JB's, the patrons created a lively and aggressive macho culture with its own norms. The scene described here captures the basic norms of the bar. It was a Thursday afternoon. There were nine patrons in the bar: six Mexicans and three whites. JB, Mr. Charlie, and Efren were playing dominoes and Raymond was watching. Leo and Juanio were at the bar talking. The white patrons were White Mike, Paul, and Kevin, who were standing at the bar, talking, and occasionally glancing at the antics going on in the game.

> Geraldo, the attorney, walks in coatless and with his tie undone. "Jayyyy Beeeee," he says in a loud voice as he approaches the domino table. "Jerrryyy," JB responds just as loudly and stands as they hug. Geraldo places some quarters on the table, shakes hands with everyone, and says, "I'm here to kick some ass, gentlemen." "The only ass you're going to see is mine," Efren says, "and only if I show you." "Well, fucker," Geraldo responds, "you better be ready to show it." He then walks down the bar shaking hands with the patrons, saying, "How are you doing, fellows?" He goes behind the bar, prepares a bucket of beer, opens the register, and places some money in one of the troughs and takes out some change. He places the bucket of beer on the bar, takes one out, and tells everyone "help yourself fellows" as he heads toward the domino table. "Get ready for an ass-kicking, gentlemen," he tells the players as he sits down.

The norms illustrated in this scenario were the shaking of hands, drinking, symbolic ownership of the bar, profanity, teasing, and gambling, and they were the primary rituals in the bar.

Shaking Hands

The shaking of hands is a social act that involves two people extending their right hands, clasping them together, and pumping up and down. The practice originated among males to illustrate they did not have a weapon in their hands (Hall and Spencer Hall 1983). Today, depending upon the social context the handshake can be a symbol of congratulations, reconciliation, gratitude, condolences, or a way to say hello or goodbye. Regardless of the context, the handshake is an affirmation of friendship. When the patrons first entered JB's, as Geraldo illustrated, they walked through the bar and affirmed their friendships by shaking hands with those present. The handshake was usually accompanied by phrases such as "Heyyyyy, where you been," "how have you been," "what's up," "good to see you," or "what's going on?" Often the greeting came with an offer of beer and an invitation to join the group. Sometimes the patrons hugged, as illustrated by JB and Geraldo. This was more personal than a handshake because it involved more bodily contact.

JB was especially diligent in shaking everyone's hand and he apologized when he failed to do so. When a patron left the bar, the common pattern was to shake hands with his immediate group and perhaps wave at everyone else. The goodbye handshake came with comments and questions such as "see you later" or "you are leaving already?" "be careful" "see you the next time" or "take care of yourself." The handshake is so culturally ingrained and mundane that it is easy to overlook its significance. Note, for example, that to refuse to shake someone's hand is an insult and could lead to conflict. If the handshake was not important culturally it would not be so ubiquitous and repeated so often (Wierzbicka 1995; Hall and Spencer Hall 1983). What was notable about JB's was that friendship via the handshake was expressed among the same group of people daily. There are not many places in society where this is such a common occurrence.

Drinking

There are many reasons why people drink, such as taste, relaxation, mood alteration, food enhancement, celebrations, hospitality, and health (Heath 2000; Brodsky and Peele 1999; Peele and Grant 1999). The primary reason, however, has always been sociability, the opportunity to interact with friends (Oldenburg 1989). This explains why the patrons visited JB's on a regular basis. Alcohol consumption increases sociability, and sociability increases alcohol consumption. No one goes to a neighborhood bar to drink alone or only to drink. One can drink alone at home. People go to bars to find companionship and engage in conversation. Drinking is the lubricant for talking, and the talking/drinking combination is the foundation of neighborhood bars like JB's with conversation the main activity. When asked in a survey why they consumed alcohol, the two most common reasons given by Mexican men were to relax, talk, and loosen up around people (Golding et al. 1992).

Drinking in JB's was facilitated by several factors. One, it was a male gathering place and males tend to drink more when they are part of a group, especially if the group consists of long-standing friends, which was the case with JB's. Drinking in a group creates and reproduces solidarity. Two is the macho code (Panitz et al. 1983). It is manly to drink, and if the occasion calls for it, to drink a lot. A real man can "hold his liquor," meaning that one can maintain control even during heavy drinking. Three was the bucket culture in JB's. Patrons could purchase a bucket of six beers for the price of five. They ordered buckets with the intention of sharing the beer with others, as Geraldo illustrated in the example. If your brand was not in the bucket, you could ask JB to "trade it out" for your preference, a common practice. Often the bar and floor of the deck were covered with full, half-full, or empty buckets. When someone arrived and joined the group, they usually bought a bucket and placed it among the others as Jerry did. This was reciprocity, the ritual way of treating the group as one had been treated. "JB, give us a bucket" was a common refrain in the bar.

Symbolic Ownership

Drinking in a group on a regular basis not only facilitates cohesion, it also creates an emotional attachment to the social space within which it occurs (Cavan 1966). Many of JB's regulars said it was the only place where they drank and called it "my home away from home" or "our bar" and "our place." Several said they had spent so much money at JB's over the years they felt like they owned a "piece of the place." Harvey said that at one time he was spending so much time at JB's that his wife asked why he did not move there. "I would if I could," he told her, "but JB doesn't have closet space or a bedroom." The most significant manifestation of collective ownership in JB's was the practice of the patrons going behind the bar and retrieving their own beer. Many times, a patron would walk in, greet everyone, then go behind the bar and retrieve a beer or fill a bucket without JB's knowledge because he was reading the paper, engaged in a conversation, paying bills, playing dominoes, or outside on the deck. Patrons would then seek JB and pay, or pay before they left. Often patrons would tell JB they were going behind the bar to retrieve beer or JB would tell a customer to get his own beer. Others like Geraldo retrieved their own beer without saying anything to JB and paid before they left. Some patrons, also like Geraldo, used the cash register, made their own change, and served other customers. On some occasions JB left the bar to run errands and would tell the patrons to "fend for yourselves until I get back." When this happened, someone would go behind the bar, serve others, and use the cash register, or everyone would retrieve their own beer and pay JB when he returned. This does not mean that JB never tended to his bar, for indeed he did. The point is that the norm of patrons getting their own beer, coupled with JB's trust, reinforced the idea that the bar was a collective enterprise symbolically owned by everyone, and it worked because everyone adhered to the norm. Initially, I thought that only JB's closest friends went behind the bar, but it quickly became apparent that all but a few patrons did so. The new patrons also retrieved their own beer. Paul, for example, was one of the white coworkers that White Mike introduced to the bar during the study. Initially he did not go behind the bar to retrieve his own beer. One day when JB was outside on the deck,

Paul asked White Mike, who was engaged in another conversation, to "get me a beer." "I'm busy," White Mike responded, "you can get it; here everyone gets their own beer." After some hesitation, Paul went behind the bar and retrieved a beer and he continued to do so thereafter whenever he was in the bar. Another example was Louis, another white coworker brought to the bar by White Mike. Louis only frequented the bar for a short period of time, but by his third visit, he was going behind the bar and getting beer for himself and others. The few patrons who did not go behind the bar did so out of their own volition, as Manuel, a former bar owner, made clear one afternoon. JB was hosting a barbecue and Manuel and I were standing at the bar talking. Most of the patrons, including JB, were out on the deck drinking beer and eating barbecue. We watched as several people walked in and went behind the bar to retrieve beers or fill a bucket and go back outside to the deck. Manuel looked at me, shook his head, and made the following comments:

> "You know I've been in the bar business most of my life and I have prob-
> ably been in every bar in Northside and many others in Houston, but I
> have never been in a place where customers go behind the bar and get
> their own beer. It's the damnest thing I've ever seen; I tell you I sure as hell
> wouldn't allow it if I still had the Players' Lounge. No way in hell I would
> let customers go behind the bar, but here everybody does it." "Do you ever
> go behind the bar?" I ask. "Oh, hell no," he responds. "I don't believe in it.
> I don't think JB would mind, you know, but I don't want to. I don't even
> think about it."

JB said that the practice began a few years after he opened the bar. A group of patrons worked the night shift and sought a place where they could drink beer when they got off work in the morning. Initially JB opened for them, but he grew tired of getting up early after going to bed late and decided to loan them a key. He trusted them because they were longtime friends from Second Ward. The men opened the bar in the morning, sat outside at the table in the vacant lot, kept track of how much beer they consumed, and then settled with JB later. JB said they always paid for the beer they consumed and that he never had any problems with the arrangement. When these same patrons visited the bar during regular hours, they continued to go behind the bar for their beer. JB often joined them at the outside tables and they would pay him for a round and go inside to retrieve their beer. The practice eventually spread to other customers and it became the norm. One patron told me that he believed that people took advantage of the practice and drank free. "I've seen them do it," he said. Other patrons disagreed. When I asked Geraldo, he emphatically replied, "No one rips anybody off. In here we're family." Leo echoed the sentiment. "We may forget to pay for a beer or two along the way," he said, "but no one does it intentionally, and if they do and we find out about it we'll run their ass off." Not once during the study did JB and a customer disagree over the practice, and I never heard JB tell someone they could not go behind the bar and get a beer. When I asked him about this norm, he made the following comment:

> "I know everyone who comes in here, most of them for a long time. If they want to rip me off, they can because I tend to trust everyone because I know them, but I don't think they do, really, I never worry about it. It's never been an issue."

Profanity

The topics discussed in the bar varied, but regardless of the subject, profanity was part of the patrons' vocabulary. Profanity has usually been the norm in neighborhood bars but rarely ever recorded by those who have researched drinking establishments. In a study of a Midwestern bar, the author stated in the preface that he omitted the obscenities uttered by the patrons because "I do not think they would want all their expressions to appear in print" (LeMasters 1975). The taboo nature of profanity explains why it has not been a major topic of research interest (Jay 2000, 1992). It is aggressive, crude, vulgar, and seen as the language of the underworld, the backstage, the locker room, and social spaces of play like JB's. However, it was such a prominent part of the patrons' speech that it could not be ignored because of the function it served. It is one of the ways by which the patrons expressed aggression. Indeed, profanity is the language of aggression. It reinforces and reproduces notions of toughness, a trait that defines manhood (Perinbanayagam 2000). Note, for example, that men generally curse more than women and use more offensive terms (Jay 1992). Profanity is also a male bonding mechanism. It is their special argot and a symbol of the camaraderie and equality that exists among them as men. Profanity is usually not taken literally because such interpretations for the most part are absurd and thus not their intent. Rather, profane words are used for emphasis and to make strong statements. The words fuck and fucking, the profane words most often uttered in the bar, were used in a nonsexual sense 87 percent of the time, as is usually the situation (Sheidlower 1999). "Fuck you" was used to tell a person to go to hell, and "don't fuck with me" meant that one did not want to engage in or put up with joking. It also stressed difficulty, as when a pipe fitter said he used the biggest wrench he could find on "that fucking pipe" to break it loose, or emphasized excessive drinking, as in "I got fucked up last night." The word motherfucker is the most offensive profane word in the English language because it suggests incest with one's mother, the most aberrant form of sexual deviancy. When a patron called someone a motherfucker, it meant that his behavior was equal to or below that of a sexual deviant. The term was even once used for emphasis in a positive sense, when one patron described a new coworker as "a pretty good motherfucker."

The excessive use of profanity in JB's did not escape attention. Some patrons had a reputation for not being able to carry on a conversation without using profanity. One college-educated patron, for example, had a reputation for excessive profanity. Once, after uttering a string of expletives, another patron asked why he cursed so much. "Because I fucking want to," he responded. "You may want to," he was told, "but it doesn't become you." The patron did not respond. In another instance, a patron after hearing another patron spew several profanities turned to me and said, "You know I never hear that kind of language unless I come in here." At times, the cursing exchanges were comical. One of the regular patrons walked into the bar one afternoon and joined his friends sitting at the bar.

"I'm sure glad you found that welder," the newly arrived patron was told by another patron. "Man you were getting on everybody's ass because you thought somebody stole it. Hell, you even called and started cursing me." "You motherfucker, I did not," the patron emphatically responded. Everyone laughed. "Man, that's classic," another patron observed.

In another instance a patron was cursing profusely when another patron said, "You know, you have a limited vocabulary." "Fuck you," the patron responded. "I rest my case," the criticizing patron retorted, to laughter. Yet, despite these sentiments, the profanity was commonplace and as such, it tended to lose its sting given that it was used so often in a casual manner. Nevertheless, the context could quickly surround the profanity with drama.

Teasing

The teasing in the bar was a source of much entertainment. It was how the patrons sparred, competed, and displayed wit and quick thinking. Like profanity, the teasing episodes were an expression of male solidarity because they generated group laughter and reinforced friendships and bonding. As an interaction form, however, teasing contains a duality. On the one hand, it is a mock insult designed to generate laughter and hence cohesion, but on the other hand it is an act of aggression that can quickly and easily get out of hand and become a serious insult (Ziv 2010; Pawluk 1989). The border between the two sides of teasing therefore is fluid, and often the teasing exists in the borderlands. Although instances of teasing gone awry were recorded, most of the teasing was accepted and given and taken as acts of playful behavior. The patrons teased each other about everything, including work, personal habits, sex, drinking, friends, family, domino skills, and race. Although the teasing may have irritated, stung, and embarrassed, as I experienced firsthand, a patron who could not endure teasing would probably not be a patron very long, for it was an entrenched norm, and most if not all the regular patrons at one time or another were teased and some more than others. Indeed, the prominence of teasing is obvious in the chapters that follow. Again, the teasing reflected the friendship between the patrons, for only friends could tease other friends in an aggressive manner and remain friends. Consider the following two episodes. In the first, I was the teased. I was standing at the bar with a group of patrons watching the domino game when the following ensued.

> "Do you know anything about real estate?" Efren asks me. His question catches me off guard. "A little bit," I respond, "why do you ask?" Efren turns his chair towards me, spreads his legs, grabs his testicles, and asks, "Is this a lot?" Everyone howls and laughs loudly. I feel my ears turn red as I laugh and wait out the laughter of the others. "I walked into that one," I say. "A whole lot of love in here tonight," Efren responds.

In the second example, the octogenarian Mr. Charlie was the object of teasing, and he retorted in a manner that defused the attack and gave him the upper hand in the exchange. Mr. Charlie was playing dominoes with Leo, JB, and Kid. Several patrons were standing and sitting at the bar watching the game.

> "Hey Mr. Charlie," Leo asks, "do you ever miss it?" "Do I ever miss what?" Mr. Charlie asks. "You know, being with a woman, do you remember how it used to feel?" There is some chuckling. Mr. Charlie pauses for a moment and then asks, "How you know what I can and cannot feel?" "Because you can't find it anymore," Leo says to laughter. "How do you know?" Mr. Charlie asks. He pauses and then continues, "and just for your information, I still have a lot of dick." We laugh. He pauses again for effect and then says, "and I still get quite a few compliments on it too." The patrons howl and laugh.

Teasing as a form of microaggression has the potential to become an insult and cause serious resistance. In the following example, the teased felt the teaser overstepped the boundary of what was acceptable. He rejected the joke, which in turn required private emotional work on the part of the teaser to repair the friendship. What magnified the event was that the patrons involved were good friends. There were several other patrons present, and the content of their teasing dealt with girlfriends, past and present, and who gained and lost with girlfriends.

"Shit," a patron tells another patron, "all your girlfriends were ugly, and I mean really ugly." Everyone laughs except the teased, and as the laughter subsides the teased replies in a stern manner. "I don't appreciate your comments, you're talking about the mother of my children." The bar goes quiet. "Hey, I didn't mean anything," the teaser responds. There are a few moments of silence. Some patrons look away and others start their own conversations. After a few seconds, the teaser approaches the teased, speaks to him quietly, and they walk outside. They obviously reconciled for they reenter the bar 15 minutes later laughing and joking.

Gambling

There were three forms of gambling in the bar: the 8 Liners, pots, and dominoes. Gambling creates a sense of action and this was most evident in the domino games. The 8 Liners functioned like slot machines in that one puts money into a machine and wins through capturing the same icon across or up and down a screen by pushing buttons, rather than pulling down a lever as one does with true slot machines. The winners received tickets that spewed out from a slot near the bottom of the machine that JB redeemed for beer. The 8 Liners machines belonged to Manuel and he split the money the patrons put into the machines with JB. JB once mentioned that the 8 Liners generated less money now than in the past. Nevertheless, several of the players put up to $60 or more in the 8 Liners in one sitting. Panchito appeared in my notes thirty-eight times, and during each visit, he spent the entire time playing the 8 Liner. If he ran out of money, he would borrow from JB, and on more than one occasion Panchito would enter the bar, pay JB the money he owed him, play the 8 Liner, lose, and reborrow the money. Some of the players would talk to the machine, cursing or praising it. One evening Chulo Culo (Cute Ass) played the 8 Liner for several hours and cursed it as he was losing. When his losses reached $300, he lost his temper and attacked the machine by kicking it and hitting it with his fist.

JB also sponsored a money pot for the Super Bowl, Pro Bowl, and for meat. The meat pot was a weekly affair, and winners won a variety of meats provided by Willie the Butcher, one of the Mexican patrons. Often the winner donated the meat to the bar for grilling. The Super Bowl pot was the most prominent because of the amount of money involved. JB had been sponsoring it for as long as he'd had the bar, and a large majority of people who purchased the squares had been doing so for years. Many made payments toward their square throughout the year, and JB had a waiting list of those who wanted to participate. Other patrons who sponsored football pots marveled at JB's loyal players. "He doesn't have to go out and collect his money," they commented, "they come here and pay." This loyalty was magnified one afternoon as we were playing dominoes.

> A woman, her daughter, and granddaughter walk in. The game stops as JB stands and greets them with hugs. They gather at the other end of the bar where they speak in hushed tones. We hear muffled crying. JB again hugs the woman. After speaking again in hushed tones, they leave and JB rejoins the game. "What was that about?" Manuel asks. "The woman's husband passed away a few weeks ago," JB says, "and one of his last requests was that she keep his square on my Super Bowl pot. He's had that square ever since I've been running the pot, and he was afraid he would lose it when he died. She came by to make a payment."

The week before the Super Bowl game, JB hosted a barbecue and drew the numbers for the pot. People arrived early to drink, eat, and socialize. At 5 p.m. JB drew and announced the numbers one by one and placed them on the pot's grid, first across the top and then down the left side. When he finished, he made copies and passed them out to the players, so they could find their names on the grid. Loud and simultaneous talk followed as people praised or damned their possibilities of winning. Many patrons remained after the drawing and continued drinking, eating, and socializing.

The third form of gambling and the most dominant type was the domino game. It was the most entertaining because it involved the players interacting with each other. Playing the 8 Liner involved interacting with a machine, and purchasing a square on a pot allowed one to compete for the "luck of the draw" with a silent and largely unseen collectivity. The playing of dominoes was different because it was played most days, required face-to-face interaction, and was played in an aggressive manner on a small table. This made it entertaining not only for the players but also for the patrons who watched the game. The game was extremely competitive and played for a quarter a hand. The players were often extremely critical of each other's plays, and their profanity-laced criticism and teasing made the patrons who were watching laugh. Learning how to play and becoming a regular player was one of the ways I became a part of the bar's community. During the game, the patrons' aggressive interactions entertained the players and those who were watching.

The Community Social Center

JB sponsored several events each year that transformed the bar from a semi-private social club for men into a social center for the community that drew family, friends, former patrons, and others from the surrounding area. Birthdays and anniversaries were the most common types of celebrations. Fundraisers were also held at the bar to raise funds for people in need, scholarships, and to support a golf tournament organized by "Phil the Thrill," one of the Mexican patrons. During these fiestas, I saw people whom I had never seen or whom I encountered only during these special occasions.

Vaquero Meetings

Several of the Mexican patrons were members of the Fort Bend Vaqueros (Cowboys), an organization that was part of a statewide network of Vaquero organizations. Their purpose was to honor and perpetuate the tradition of the Tejano vaqueros. Indeed, Tejano culture and history were important to many of the participants. The following comments about Tejano music made this apparent. Three patrons standing at the bar mourned its decline and lamented that *mayate* (slang for African American) music was being favored by the younger generations. What prompted the conversation was the Tejano music that was playing on the jukebox. The patrons were listening intently, and after a short while the following conversation took place.

> "You know," Johnny says, "Tejano music is dying. They don't play it on the radio in Houston anymore; you have to go to San Antonio or Corpus or the Valley if you want to hear it." "I know," Joe responds, "we have the fourth largest city in the nation with a lot of Tejanos and no Tejano station." "Not only that," Ramon interjects, "our people are not turning out for our Tejano stars. Hell, I went to see Little Joe and Ruben Ramos the other night and the place was half-empty." "All you hear now is that rap shit," Johnny says. "Man, I can't stand it with all the curse words and everything." "Yeah, I know," Ramon responds, "our own kids growing up on mayate music, no Tejano at all." "It's a damn shame," Joe says, "Tejano is part of our culture, of who we are." "The stations are catering to immigrants and their music because they represent a whole lot of people," Ramon says. "It's still a damn shame," Joe answers.

The local Vaquero chapter held its meetings at JB's outside on the deck once a month, and many showed up dressed in Western gear. Upwards of fifty people would attend, and afterwards they would stay and socialize and drink beer. JB usually provided food. At least once a year, the Vaqueros rode their horses and covered wagons down the main streets in Second Ward and Magnolia Park and stopped at JB's and other bars along the way. Their big event each year was the trail ride. During the first week of March, the Vaquero organizations from across the state participated in a trail ride to Houston for the start of the annual Houston Livestock Show and Rodeo. The local Vaquero chapter drove to San Antonio and joined other Vaquero chapters, and all rode into Houston on horses and in covered wagons. The trip took two weeks, and once in Houston, all the Vaquero organizations from around the state rode their horses and covered wagons in the annual downtown parade to mark the opening of the rodeo. Afterwards many rode their horses and covered wagons to JB's for a barbecue. Usually up to a hundred people attended, and the parking lot was taken over by horses and covered wagons, and the deck and inside bar by men, women, and children dressed like cowboys and cowgirls. Many of the men wore long black dusters with the name of their organizations on the back. This event tended to draw more females than any other festivity that JB sponsored.

The Marines' Birthday

Every year on November 10th, JB hosted a party to celebrate the Marines' Birthday. The Mexican patrons were very patriotic, and many had served in the armed forces—mostly in the Marines and Army, but a few served in the Navy. JB provided the food, but often other patrons brought food and volunteered to barbecue. The patrons who served in the Marines were particularly proud of their service. JB and Leo owned black leather jackets with a large Marine insignia on the back. JB owned several sweatshirts with the Marine insignia in the center, and Leo wore a gold Marine insignia on a gold chain around his neck. There was a large picture on the wall behind the domino table with a statue of the Marines raising the flag on Iwo Jima, and there were several Marine bumper stickers on the mirror behind the bar. Weeks before the party, JB took orders from other Marine veterans for hats and T-shirts that bore the Marine insignia and slogan, *Semper Fi*, to wear during the celebration. Other patrons showed up wearing their service hats, fatigue pants, and/or shirts and medals and ribbons. Throughout the evening, they drank beer, ate, exchanged exaggerated stories about their experiences in the service, and teased each other about which branch of the service was the toughest and truly for "men."

Christmas Party

A week before Christmas, JB hosted a Christmas party. The party started late in the afternoon and lasted throughout the evening. The food usually included turkey, ham, tamales, and cold cuts. On at least two such occasions, Leo fried turkeys. During the party, many patrons talked about their Christmas plans, the gifts they bought or did not buy, and spoke nostalgically of Christmases past. One year, for example, one of the Mexican patrons told a story of how poor his family was when he was a kid. "If it wasn't for the Good Fellows," he said, "my brothers and sisters and I would not have received anything, no presents at all, nada." Another Mexican patron said the only time he ever received a gift at Christmas was when he was seven and it was a truck. "I can still see it," he said. Harvey spoke of the year the bar was open on Christmas Day. "All of the single men were here," he said, "and we ate rib eye roast. I put it on one of those slow turning rotisseries and, man, the aroma filled the whole place." JB said it was the first time he had ever opened on Christmas, and Efren, a widower, tended the bar.

Networking

It is inevitable that when the same group of people interact informally over an extended period of time, they establish a network for the transfer and flow of material and nonmaterial resources. This happened at JB's. It was a place where people purchased and exchanged services with other patrons. This included the installation of air conditioners, house remodeling, giving and receiving legal and financial advice, and buying and selling cars, golf paraphernalia, athletic apparel, bouquets of flowers, fruit trees, and meat. Some of these exchanges were gratuitous, and if a fee was involved it was often at a reduction.

Communal Eating

There was also a great deal of communal eating in the bar. Communal eating involves two pleasures, one that comes from feeling satiated, and the second from interacting and sharing with other human beings (Fernandez-Armesto 2001). There were several barbecue grills on the deck and one large grill on the right side of the deck. Often JB or Leo announced that they were going to cook in the evening, or tomorrow, or some other date. The food was always free, and the menus included chicken, fajitas, ribs, pepper steak, fish, shrimp, meat and cabbage, chili con carne, carne guisada, menudo, chili, hamburgers, and hot dogs. Flour and corn tortillas, bread, and tamales were always available. JB and Leo also volunteered to cook for special occasions such as birthdays, anniversaries, and retirements.

Outside Activities

Some of the patrons also fished and played golf with each other. The fishing trips were usually out-of-town trips that lasted several days. Some of the patrons also spoke of trips they once took together to Mexico.

In summary, several things made JB's a unique neighborhood bar. One was its small size with an official capacity of twenty-five people. This created a sense of privacy and intimacy that other, larger neighborhood bars in the area did not have. The bar's small size facilitated interaction because the patrons were physically close to each other and this made the personalities of the patrons more salient. The patrons were a unique mix of Mexican and white middle-aged men of working- and middle-class status who had known each other for a long time. The Mexican patrons were the majority and the white patrons the minority, and together they constituted a relatively closed community that can be described as a large informal clique that gathered at JB's, their semi-private bar, on a regular basis to drink, eat, relax, play dominoes, and talk and banter and tease each other. In the process, they established and reproduced their identities and friendships and created an aggressive and lively macho culture that included race talk, the primary topic covered in this narrative.

CHAPTER TWO

Mexicans vs. Whites

I t is difficult for people to talk about race when they are in the presence of another racial group for fear of saying something wrong and being accused of prejudice (Bonilla-Silva 2006). White Americans especially find it stressful to interact with other racial groups, especially with African Americans. They must exert more cognitive and affective efforts to avoid saying something inappropriate and therefore tend to avoid contact with African Americans beyond fleeting and cursory moments. When they are in the presence of other whites, however, race talk abounds (Houts Picca and Feagin 2007; Myers 2005), especially if the location is a backstage area where informality reigns. Most of it is negative, uttered by males and usually in the form of ridicule and jokes. Racial prejudice and racism among whites has not abated, as some people may believe, but has only gone underground where informality prevails and self-expressions are more candid (Bonilla-Silva 2006).

The Bar and Incongruity

Avoiding race talk was not the norm in JB's. Indeed, it was an integral part of the relationship between the Mexican and white patrons. Race may not have been the patrons' central concern, but it was ever poised to surface, and often the race talk was the focus of everyone present. Most of the patrons' racial comments occurred primarily within the context of humor. Humor is that which makes us laugh, but what is it that makes us laugh? The answer is incongruity (Kuiper 2008; Clark 1970) and in the bar it was racial incongruity. To understand how the social world works is to see things congruently. In the racial stratification system of the United States, the white population is the dominant racial group. They have more wealth, power, and prestige relative to other racial groups. To grasp this situation is to possess congruency, that is, to know that whites occupy a much higher status than Mexicans. In the bar the situation was reversed. The Mexican patrons were the numerical majority and had more power, prestige, and status, and they acted in like fashion. The white patrons were the numerical minority with less power, prestige, and status in the bar and were treated as such. This inverted social situation was the incongruity that served as the circumstance for the humorous race talk. People do not laugh at what they do not understand and JB's patrons were aware of the historical and contemporary reality of Mexican-white relations in the world outside of JB's, and they laughed when it was turned upside down in the bar.

The Dual Nature of Racial Joking

Racial joking, like joking and teasing in general, has positive and negative effects (Pawluk 1989). The positive originates from laughter because it stimulates feelings of goodwill, pulls people together, and strengthens cohesion. In JB's the laughter was accessible and contagious because it was a small bar where group laughter was the norm. The negative effects stem from the aggressive and hostile nature embedded in racial joking (Davis 1993). Someone was being belittled because of his racial affiliation. The potential for conflict therefore was always present. The humorous context, however, signaled that the belittling was not to be taken at face value because the principals involved were acting in jest and playing racial roles (Fine 1983; Stephenson 1951) and did not mean what they said. At times, however, the race talk started out humorously but then crossed the boundary into seriousness. Further, the racial comments were grounded in real-world circumstances, regardless of the context surrounding the talk. Hence, as will be discussed, they contained messages and signals that revealed hidden and repressed antagonisms.

The Appeal of JB's to the White Patrons

The freewheeling, hypermasculine, Mexican-influenced culture of the bar, where aggressive behavior and laugher was abundant, was the lure for JB's white patrons. Three regular white patrons made this apparent in their comments about why they patronized JB's.

> "I liked JB's because it was a Meskin bar," Harvey says. "I had never been around a group of men who liked each other, drank, hung out, always kidded each other and did things for one another. I don't think white people are like that, my family certainly wasn't."
>
> "I come here because everybody knows everybody," White Mike says. "Meskins like to hang out with their friends and family. Y'all are not like us, we hate our families. Hell, look at this place. There is always something going on and everybody is somehow related to everybody else and they come here every day to see each other."
>
> "I like the characters and the bullshit," Jerry tells me when I ask about his patronage of the bar. "The Meskins make me laugh. I've liked it from the first time I ever came here."

Harvey and White Mike stressed the cohesion, camaraderie, networking, and action in JB's. Everyone knew, liked, joked, and helped each other. White Mike also drew sharp distinctions between Mexican and white group values: Mexicans liked to be around their families and friends, and whites did not. Jerry highlighted the bar's entertainment value. The atmosphere of the bar allowed people to relax and be more expressive and "be who I really am." Therefore, Jerry came to the bar to see, hear, and talk with the different characters and to laugh at their bullshit, that is, to enjoy himself. The Meskins made him laugh. Bars are social spaces of play, and the white patrons obviously liked to play with the Mexicans or they would not have become regular patrons. Playing with the Mexicans, however, came with a price, i.e., being the objects of microaggressions and amusement because of their whiteness, and although they pushed back, they nevertheless were the targets more than vice versa.

Race Talk Patterns

Human behavior tends to be patterned because we are prone to do the same things repeatedly. This gives our actions a degree of predictability. Indeed, over time I could anticipate when certain racial performances would occur based upon who was in the bar. Three constant themes framed the racial interaction, though their acting out of them may have differed. One was a role reversal where the Mexican patrons played the part of the dominant majority group and whites played the role of the minority group that experienced prejudice and discrimination. These roles mocked the quota system implied by affirmative action policies. A second pattern was the Mexican patrons questioning white values and norms and positioning themselves as the superior group by using "white" as an adjective, as in "white boy." A third was the greeting between JB and Mike that involved a reference to Mike's nickname "White Mike" coupled with the term motherfucker, the most insulting and profane term in the English language. Mike allowed JB to ridicule him in this manner, but he made it clear to the white patrons that they could not address him in the same manner.

The Quota System

Affirmative action policies were devised by the U.S. government and private organizations in the 1960s to compensate for the history of racial discrimination against Mexicans, African Americans, and other historically disadvantaged populations in higher education, the upper levels of the occupational structure, and contracting (Crosby and Van DeVeer 2000). Specific quotas were illegal, but affirmative action policies nevertheless received criticisms as quota systems because they required consideration of minority applicants (Newport 2016). The policies were controversial because they ran counter to America's ideology of merit, the idea that college admissions and hiring should depend upon qualifications and that race should not be a criterion. Whites felt pushed aside unfairly and began filing discrimination suits arguing that less-credentialed nonwhites received preference and hence they were victims of reverse discrimination. Yet, despite some setbacks, affirmative action policies remain in operation in American society. The city of Houston, for example, has a set-aside program that ensures that minority-owned firms receive a fair share of city contracts when the city purchases goods and services. Also, universities in Houston and elsewhere in the nation have devised admission policies that take a variety of factors into consideration, including race.

In the bar, both the Mexican and white patrons mocked these policies as a quota system, and they did so with glee. The Mexicans told the white patrons that JB's had a quota and only a set number of whites could be in the bar at any given time. The white patrons went along with the ruse by playing the role of the aggrieved minority that only sought equal treatment. The idea of a white quota ironically came from Harvey, one of the white patrons. At one time, a group of white judges and lawyers patronized the bar, and Harvey said sometimes he would walk into the bar and "it would be full of whites."

"The draw for me was that JB's was a Meskin bar, but there for a while I was worried and had my doubts," Harvey tells me. "Hell, they used to call me the token white, but sometimes there would be just as many whites as

Meskins in the bar so, hell, I told JB that we needed a quota system that only so many whites could be in the bar at any given time and that's how it got started. Hell, I didn't want JB's to turn into a white bar."

Harvey wanted whites to continue to be a numeric minority in the bar even though he was teased as being a token. He did not want it to become a white bar because he feared it would lose what made it attractive to him, the company of Mexican men and the camaraderie he found there. His affection for the place and its patrons was obvious. At times there were as many whites in the bar as Mexicans, but usually the Mexican patrons were in the majority and everyone went along with the charade of a quota. When leaving, for instance, some white patrons would finish their beer and then say, "I have to go. We are over our white quota anyway" or "There are too many white people in here." These comments always brought chuckles. The quota scenario was also played out in larger and longer performances. One afternoon Manuel, JB, Efren, and Mr. Charlie were playing dominoes. Harvey, White Mike, Crash, Ramon, Leo, Ruben, and I were watching the game from the bar. Manuel, Harvey, and White Mike were the only white patrons present when Mr. Jim came hobbling in with his cane through the Canal Street door.

"Oh, hell," JB says, feigning disgust. "You can't come in because we already have our quota of white people; you'll have to wait outside until someone leaves." We laugh. "You can never have too many white people," Mr. Jim says hobbling by the table towards the other end of the bar. "The hell we can't," JB replies; "every time you come in there's one white person too many." We laugh again. "I'm not white," Mr. Jim responds, "I'm Polish." "Hell, that's worse," JB says. More laughter. The Canal Street door opens again and Jerry walks in. "Oh shit," JB tells him, "I should have known that once your brother was here that you would come in too." "What brother?" Jerry asks. "I don't have a brother." "Oh yes you do," JB says, "and he's sitting over there." He points to Mr. Jim. "That's not my fucking brother," Jerry says in an irritated tone. "Oh yes, he is," JB continues, "he's your white brother because all whites look alike." Everyone laughs. "Fuck you,

JB," Jerry responds. He stands at the bar with a fistful of dollars in his hand and after a few seconds asks out loud, "Can a white man get a beer around here?" "There you go," JB responds, "I let your white ass come in here and now you want me to sell you beer too." "White people only want equality," Jerry responds. Everyone is chuckling. "I'll get it," Leo tells JB and he goes behind the bar and prepares the bucket. Jerry hands Leo the money, takes the bucket, walks to the back table, and sits down alone. After a few more hands, the game stops when JB goes outside to take a phone call. "Why are you sitting alone?" Leo asks Jerry. "White people must sit in the back, especially in this place," he says with a smile on his face. Everyone laughs. JB returns and the game resumes. After a while, Jerry grabs his bucket of beer and walks outside. Approximately ten minutes later the game ends when Mr. Charlie leaves to pick up the Squealers, the name he uses to refer to his great-grandchildren. I walk out to the deck to see what is going on. All the patrons sitting on the deck—Tina, Mike, Jerry, Paul, and Kevin—are white. I greet everyone and ask, "Why you are out here by yourselves?" "This is the white people's section," White Mike says to chuckles. "Oh, do I have to be white to join you," I ask? "No, we'll let you," he says, "we don't discriminate." Everyone laughs.

The real-world circumstances surrounding quota systems were mockingly reversed. The Mexicans were "acting" like the dominant group and allowing only a certain number of whites in the bar. Whites were acting like the minority who faced and struggled against racial discrimination. When the quota was met, other whites seeking entry into the bar had to wait outside until a vacancy occurred. The size of the quota was in dispute. Indeed, one white patron in the bar was said by JB, the Mexican quota master, to be one too many, but Mr. Jim said that there could never be enough whites, an assertion that was met with resistance and ridicule. Mr. Jim also tried to justify his entering the bar at any time by removing himself from the white category and passing as Polish, a classification that was deemed worse because the Polish, JB implied, were an inferior group within the white race. In his retorts and actions, Jerry illustrated rebellion as well as compliance. He seemed truly aggravated when told that he was Mr. Jim's brother because all whites looked alike, but he jokingly complained about receiving poor service because of his whiteness. JB agreed with his assessment and warned him about overreaching, to which Jerry mockingly declared that all he wanted was equal treatment. Upon receiving his beer, he sat in the back area of the bar because whites were required to sit in the back. Later he joined the others outside on the deck, the white people's section. Whites in the bar had to sit in segregated areas just like Mexicans did in the past, and they bonded as a result just like the Mexicans. Everyone knew their roles, the afflicted and aggrieved white minority and the dominant Mexican majority, and they had learned them well. This incongruity created the circumstances for Jerry to be the victim of JB's microaggressions and it created a distorted reality that mocked real-world circumstances. It was a consistent theme that caused the patrons to smile and laugh.

Another example of Jerry being the victim of microaggressions at the hands of JB occurred one afternoon. As I approached the deck to join the group, JB stood up, took a green plastic chair off a stack of green chairs, placed it on the floor of the deck, and began wiping the seat with a rag. Jerry was the only white patron present and he was standing.

> "Here you go, cuz, sit down," JB tells me. "Damn," Jerry says, "why don't I get that kind of treatment? It must be because I'm white." "You hit it right on the head, white boy," JB responds. "Tatcho is my people and I do what I can for my people, but you white asses have to defend for yourselves; now get a green chair and sit your white ass down and be happy that I sell you beer." We laugh. "I thought so," Jerry responds.

Superiority

Research indicates that when whites jokingly disparaged other races, they experienced feelings of pleasure and dominance expressed through laughter because it reinforced the racial boundaries and stereotypes that positioned them as superior (Zenner 1970). Do minorities also feel superior when they engage in humor that disparages whites? The research is limited. Russell Middleton (1959) found that Negroes enjoyed anti-white jokes, and Americo Paredes (1961) reported that Mexican music from the Texas-Mexico border ridiculed whites, but neither study reported if this made Negroes and Mexicans feel superior. However, if disparaging remarks followed by laughter indicate feelings of superiority, they must have felt superior when they laughed, because the relationship between the two is a human condition and not the purview of any one group. Consider a scenario that occurred on the deck. The discussion was about the various wars the United States had fought, a not infrequent topic. There were seven patrons involved, and Jerry again was the only white patron in the group. It began when Leo asserted that it was primarily Mexicans and other minorities who fought the country's wars. Gilbert followed with a comment about Mexicans being the most decorated group to come out of World War II, and he mentioned a book about Roy Benavides (2005) that described his heroics in Vietnam that earned him the Medal of Honor. Chris mentioned that his uncle was cited in a book by Raul Morin (1966), who wrote about Mexican heroes in World War II. This led to Jerry being insulted because he was white and the validity of his honorable service in Vietnam was questioned. Here is how I have it in my notes.

> "Man let me tell you," Chris interjects, "Vietnam fucked up a lot of people and I'm not talking about just being wounded I'm talking about mentally, and Jerry I'm talking about you." We laugh. "Hey, wait a minute," JB interrupts, "don't be talking about ole Jerry, he's my best and most fucked-up white customer." We laugh again. "Fuck you, JB," Jerry says.

When Chris included Jerry in his remarks, Jerry laughed along with the others, but when JB criticized him, he did not laugh but rather retorted with a "go to hell" remark using the F-word.

If disparagement of a different racial group leads to inflated feelings on the part of its perpetrators, the inference is that the Mexican patrons felt superior when they laughed. There were, however, more concrete examples of Mexicans acting superior as illustrated by their use of white as an adjective, as in "you white ass" and "white boy." The noun "boy" has been a common moniker used by whites to refer to Mexican and African American males. It was an insult because it implied that Mexican and African American males were less than men—that is, childlike with connotations of intellectual and emotional inferiority. In their use of "white boy," the Mexican patrons were conveying to the white patrons that they were somehow more deficient and vile because they were white, and though uttered with humorous intent and different degrees of intensity, the phrase nevertheless positioned the Mexican patrons as the superior group on a variety of norms. Often these microaggressions lasted only a minute or less, but there were also times when they were longer.

Authority

In the following episode, White Mike was the victim of one of JB's aggressive comments that included the phrase "white boy," which diminished White Mike's manhood after he interfered with JB's instructions to Efren. Within a span of a few seconds, JB used the phrase "white boy" three times in addressing Mike. The issue was JB's authority not only over White Mike but also over Efren, one of the Mexican patrons. He reminded both that he was the ultimate authority in the bar. In addressing Efren, however, JB did so in an affectionate manner by using the term *compadre*, meaning that Efren was a very close friend. Not so with White Mike. JB scolded Efren, but Mike was warned. JB reversed the working-class world where whites tended to have authority over Mexicans. His anger played well, and for an instant, it appeared he was indeed angry, but this did not prove to be the case. The incident occurred one afternoon. Leo, Chris, Philip, and White Mike were standing on the side of the deck watching JB cook slabs of pork ribs on a large barbecue pit hitched to a trailer. White Mike was the only white patron present. Efren came out of the bar and joined the group. He looked at the pit and said it was too high in the front and that the grease from the ribs was flowing back into the firebox causing the flames to shoot up. JB instructed Efren to lower the pit in front with the winch so the grease would drop out of the pipe and into a bucket. Efren turned the winch a couple of times when White Mike said out loud, "That's enough, stop." "No," Leo chimed in, "it needs to be turned some more." JB checked the pit and indeed the front needed more lowering.

> "Goddamn it, *compadre*," JB tells Efren, "why are you listening to that white boy? That's the last time I want you to take the word of a white boy over mine. I didn't tell you to stop, and goddamn it white boy don't be contradicting my orders to my *compadre*." We laugh. "Fuck you JB," White Mike responds. Efren turns the winch a few more times and, in a few seconds, the grease starts dripping out of the pipe and into the bucket.

Morality

Most racial groups disparage the morality of other groups. Mexicans, for example, have been described by whites as lazy, freeloaders, promiscuous, drug dealers, and illegal (*Business Insider* 2018; De Leon 1983). The morality of whites was described by the Mexicans in the bar as arrogant, self-centered, promiscuous, racist. Each group, of course, believed their morality was superior, but white morality is normative in society because of white cultural dominance. In the bar, the circumstances were reversed. The Mexicans were in control. It was their mini-society and their morality positioned as superior. Two examples follow. The first dealt with gender relations and the second with money. One afternoon Harvey began talking about a trip he was taking with his ex-wife. He was describing the condominium he rented and its wooded surroundings when Leo interrupted. Their exchanges were not meant to be funny but were infused with humor by an emphatic and loud comment made by a Mexican patron at the bar.

> "Let me get this straight, you and your ex-wife are going on a trip, right?" Leo asks Harvey. Harvey nods his head yes. "Are you going to be staying together?" Leo asks. "She will be in the same condo," Harvey responds. "You see that's a white people thing, only white people do these things," Leo replies in animated manner. "Mexicans would never think of staying

with their ex-wives anywhere." "YEAH, WHAT'S WRONG WITH YOU?" someone asks Harvey from the bar in a loud, emphatic, and mock tone of indignation. Everyone laughs.

In using the phrase "white people thing," Leo was alleging that the behavior in question was a distinct and negative feature of white culture in comparison with Mexican culture. Hence, Mexicans would never consort with their ex-wives—that's a "thing" white people do. A "thing" is an object and its use by Leo objectified the white norm of consorting with ex-wives and made it sound impersonal. In Mexican culture, by contrast, a man would never do that. This was not true, of course, and the final emphatic statement—"what's wrong with you"—made everyone laugh because it implied if Harvey acted more like a Mexican and did not consort with his ex-wife, he would be considered a better person. This made the audience laugh because Mexican males are not "holier than thou," especially Leo, who had been married five times and whose favorite saying was "I don't cheat on my wife or my girlfriend." There is, of course, no cultural proscription among Mexicans against having contact with ex-spouses. Leo alleged it to be the situation so he could criticize white culture. Leo was not trying to be funny, but he and Harvey laughed along with the others when the remarks came from the patron at the bar.

The second incident was a brief exchange that occurred one afternoon. Geraldo was talking about his Easter weekend. He said he purchased a brisket special at the supermarket that included potato salad, barbecue sauce, and coleslaw and he brought the coleslaw to the bar.

"I liked everything except the coleslaw," Geraldo says. "And now you want JB to buy or raffle it," Harvey chimes in. Everyone laughs. "No," Geraldo responds in a matter-of-fact tone. "I'm not trying to make any money off of it, that's white boy stuff, but you're in the hood now." Harvey did not respond.

"In the hood" was the euphemism for the Mexican part of town and its cultural norms, where making money at every opportunity was not one of them. "That's white boy stuff," Geraldo said, a regularity that was implied to be of lesser value in comparison to Mexican norms. The term "stuff" has a variety of meanings, e.g., indeterminate or worthless. Within context the exchange spoke to the essence of different values, and Geraldo in a straightforward manner positioned "in the hood" values as superior to white values. He was a Mexican and his food was for sharing, not for selling.

White Trailer Trash

"White trailer trash" refers to poor, uneducated whites who live in trailer parks (Newitz and Wray 1997). It is a widely known slur that debases lower-class whites, especially the use of the abbreviated phrase "white trash." Trailer trash, in a generic sense, refers to anyone living in a trailer camp, regardless of race, but the combination of the three terms "white trailer trash" does not have a Mexican or black counterpart. Mexican and black trailer trash are not part of the popular vernacular. The Mexican patrons used the phrase "white trailer trash" to describe some of the patrons. The following example occurred over a two-day period. It began late one evening while we were playing dominoes. The bar was full, and several whites were present. White Mike walked in and began shaking hands with everyone at the table. He was wearing a T-shirt and blue jeans that were usually soiled from his work as a pipe fitter, but not this night. His T-shirt and blue jeans were clean, and he was wearing a head bandana with an American flag design. He appeared freshly bathed and shaved and gave off a fragrance of cologne.

> "Damn," Leo says as he and White Mike shake hands, "you smell like a Mexican, not like white trailer trash." We laugh. "Fuck you Leo," White Mike responds as he moves on and continues shaking hands with the other patrons. The next afternoon White Mike walks into the bar wearing a T-shirt and blue jeans that are dirty from working. "See," Leo tells him, "now you smell like the white trailer trash you really are." Everyone laughs. "Fuck you, Leo," White Mike again responds.

Leo not only placed White Mike among the white trailer trash, he used odor as a marker of Mexican-white differences. When White Mike walked into the bar appearing freshly bathed and perfumed, he was not reflecting his class origins but, according to Leo, was imitating a Mexican, who by comparison was the opposite of white trailer trash, i.e., they were clean and smelled good. The next day when White Mike appeared in the bar with his clothes dirty from working, Leo told him that he now reflected his status as member of the white trailer trash. Leo inverted the stereotype of the dirty Mexican and the pristine white and positioned Mexicans above whites on a social-class and hygiene hierarchy. White Mike's response in both instances was to keep walking while uttering a casual "go to hell," using the F-word. He did not participate in the laugher that Leo's remarks generated.

Another exchange that involved Leo and the phrase "white trailer trash" occurred in a discussion about whites and minorities fighting in Vietnam. A small group was sitting on the deck and once again were discussing Mexicans fighting in America's wars when the fighting in Vietnam came up. Jerry was the only white patron present.

"I don't mean to say anything negative because you're white," Leo says to Jerry, "but who do you think the officers were in Vietnam?" "They were white," Gilbert interjects quickly, "hell, everybody knows that." "Right," Leo responds, "but the soldiers doing the fighting were us, Mexicans and blacks." "Hey," JB interrupts, "you mean ole Jerry here has been lying all this time about being wounded and winning medals and all that shit?" Everyone including Jerry laughs. "Oh, I was wounded in combat all right and I have the evidence to prove it," he says, pointing to his paralyzed arm. "There were white boys like Jerry who fought," Leo continues, "you know, white trailer trash, but most of the fighting was done by us." Everyone including Jerry laughs at Leo's remarks. "I have the evidence of what I did," Jerry says again. "Vietnam fucked up a lot of people's minds," Chris chimes in, "I mean really fucked them up." "What are you trying to say about my white trailer trash friend Jerry?" JB asks again in a mock serious tone. Everyone laughs again.

The exchange began with Leo's incongruity. He did not intend to say anything negative about Jerry's whiteness but then proceeded to call him white trash as he touted the Mexicans' and blacks' combat experience. He placed Jerry within the lower class of society's hierarchy and this led to more criticisms. Chris implied that Jerry was mentally unstable while JB mockingly continued to describe Jerry in the same manner as Leo, placing Jerry as a member of the trailer trash class.

Prestige

One evening there were four Mexican patrons in the bar, myself, JB, Geraldo, and Leo, and three white patrons, Manuel, Mike, and Harvey. JB was behind the bar and the rest of us were standing at the bar. The door opened and Manuel's white friend, Billy, walked in.

> "Hey Billy," Manuel says, "how are you doing?" "Fine," Billy answers taking the stool next to Manuel. "Hey," Geraldo says from the other end of the bar, "we're going to be outnumbered." "Yeah," JB says, "what the hell is going on, this is a Mexican bar, there are too many whites in here." "Yeah and we're bringing some class to the place," Harvey retorts. "Yeah," JB responds, "some low class." Everyone laughs.

The interaction had a tone of mock seriousness. A white patron defended a violation of the quota system by claiming that white patrons brought class to the bar, implying that it lacked class because it was a Mexican bar. Since whites had more racial prestige than Mexicans did, their presence brought more prestige to the bar. The more whites you had in a Mexican bar the more prestige it had. Taken to its logical conclusion, a Mexican bar with a totally white clientele would bring the most "class." JB, however, undermined the notion of white superiority by referencing the lower-class origins of the white patrons. More whites meant more lower-class patrons and hence less prestige, a reminder of the racial hierarchy in the bar where Mexicans held more status because it was their bar.

Competence

Once, the intellectual and emotional attributes of Mexicans were judged inferior because they were half-breeds—that is, a mixture of Indian and Spanish blood (Blanton 2000; De Leon 1983; Vaca 1970). This purportedly diluted their innate capabilities. Whites, by comparison, were racially pure and hence more intelligent and emotionally mature. They were, in other words, a superior race. These genetic explanations were used to justify the exploitation of the nonwhite races, and though these notions no longer held prominent public sway, there were many who continued to believe that innate intellectual differences existed and that IQ test results reflected these differences (Herrnstein and Murray 1994). A reversal of these assertions occurred in the bar, with the Mexicans implying they were innately the superior race. This came to the fore regarding the bar's roof. It was old and flat and tended to leak whenever it rained, causing JB to place buckets on the floor to catch the dripping water. The solution was to replace the roof, but JB did not want to stand the expense because he was planning to retire in a few years. Jerry repaired the roof, but when it rained it continued to leak, and this resulted in the continuous teasing of Jerry about his competence and the quality of his work. The patrons said that when it started to rain, Jerry left, or if it was raining, Jerry would not come to the bar. The following episode began with sexual comments about a woman who had visited the bar the day before and it segued into remarks about Jerry's manhood and competence. On the deck with Jerry were JB, Leo, Rick, Duck, and Geraldo. Jerry was the only white patron.

> "Oh man, was she tall," Jerry says. "She was about six feet three . . ." "And quite good-looking," Leo chimes in. "Yeah," Jerry continues, "I was sitting at the bar and she was standing behind me and when I turned around, I was looking right at her navel." We laugh. "Man, I would like to kiss her up one leg right up to her—" "Can you do it better than fixing roofs?" JB asks, interrupting Jerry. We laugh. "Man, I told you how difficult it is to repair flat roofs," Jerry says defensively. "Well I got it fixed and my man didn't have any problem," JB responds. "That's because he's a Mexican."

"Fuck you Leo," Jerry says. "It's true, it took a Mexican to fix it; we all know whites ain't got it up here," Leo says tapping his head. Everyone but Jerry is smiling.

JB and Leo used Jerry's whiteness to question his sexual prowess by comparing it to his failed attempt to fix the roof. If Jerry could not fix roofs, how could he be a successful sexual being? Incompetence in one area implied flaws in other areas. When Jerry cited difficulty in fixing flat roofs as his defense, Leo implied it had nothing to do with difficulty. Rather, Jerry's whiteness was the reason for his incompetence, and since Mexicans were inherently more competent, it took a Mexican to fix the roof. Jerry did not participate in the laughter and responded to Leo in familiar fashion by telling him to go to hell using the F-word.

Another incident that implied innate Mexican superiority dealt with White Mike. He was tending the bar while JB was playing dominoes. There were eleven patrons—six Mexicans and five whites—present. Mike was filling the coolers with beer when he accidently knocked over an ice chest.

"Goddamn it," he says, walking out from behind the bar and kicking the ice chest towards the Drennen Street entrance along the way. "What happened?" JB asks as White Mike walks towards the Men's restroom, "and where are you going?" "To get the goddamn mop," White Mike says. "He knocked over one of the ice chests," Dale says, "and water's all over the floor." JB gets up to inspect. "Goddamn it," he says, "I let that white boy run things for a while and he fucks it up." "Fuck you, JB," Mike says as he walks out of the bathroom with a mop. He starts mopping behind the bar and knocks another ice chest over. "Goddamn," Gilbert says, "not even Efren does that." We laugh. "That's because Efren's a Mexican," JB says. "White boys can't do shit, it doesn't matter how much we teach them." We laugh again. "Fuck you, JB," White Mike says. "It's true," JB responds.

White Thing

Mores are minor norms whose violations incur light sanctions, if any. In one instance, Jerry did not say goodbye when leaving a group with whom he had been talking. The Mexican patrons speculated that his behavior reflected a "white thing," implying that in Mexican culture departing a group without saying goodbye was a violation of etiquette. Again, a white "thing" meant a characteristic that was impersonal. The group included Jerry, Benny, Ramon, and Gilbert who were standing at the bar talking. Tina was standing behind them playing the 8 Liner. Jerry and Tina were the only white patrons present. The scenario began when Tina announced that she was leaving. "That's it for me," she said and grabbed her purse and headed for the door. Jerry quickly gulped his beer and likewise headed for the door, presumably to see if he could encounter Tina.

> "Hey, are you leaving?" Benny asks. Jerry turns around quickly, says "Yeah," and walks out the door. "Damn," Benny says, "he was going to leave without telling us goodbye." "I know," Gilbert responds, "Manuel does it all the time. He will stand at the bar, drink and talk with you for an hour or so, and before you know it he walks out without telling anyone see you later or anything. I tell you he does it all of the time." "It must be a white thing, Benny replies." Everyone laughs. "It is," Gilbert says, "we would never do that."

Perhaps expressions of Mexican superiority in the bar should not be surprising given that it was a Mexican bar, owned by a Mexican and located in a Mexican part of Houston. Given this Mexican *ambiente* and the machismo that prevailed among the patrons, perhaps it would have been surprising if such feelings were not normative given the continuous presence of the white patrons, the informal atmosphere of the bar, and the history of Mexican-white relations.

JB and White Mike

Joking relationships can be symmetrical or asymmetrical, and in the bar, they were usually asymmetrical, with the Mexican patrons having the upper hand. They consistently exhibited a dominant position through their joking interactions with the white patrons. The most unusual example was the greeting between JB and White Mike. Mike received his nickname, "White Mike," during a time when three other Mikes, all Mexicans, patronized the bar. Each had a nickname so that the patrons knew which Mike was being addressed or talked about. Thus, there was Mike the Jeweler, Mike the Vaquero, Mike the Constable, and White Mike. JB's greeting usually occurred when Mike walked into the bar for the first time each day. "White Mike," he would say in a loud voice, "you goat-smelling motherfucker." At times JB would only say "White Mike," and other times only "goat smeller," but for the most part the greeting included the entire phrase. Mike's usual response was to reply in a casual fashion, "Fuck you JB," or he ignored it.

The nickname "White Mike" garnered attention because it rhymed and emphasized Mike's whiteness and publicly turned it into his master status, the one that overrode all his other statuses, such as patron, friend, pipe fitter, deer hunter, husband, father, etc. JB's greeting, however, went beyond just telling the audience that Mike was "a white person." It also described what kind of white person he was, one who smelled like a goat and had sex with his mother, the most deviant form of sexual behavior. The first time I heard JB use the phrase, it stunned because it sounded so offensive and I closely watched Mike's reaction. It was a muted "Fuck you." Other times White Mike ignored the greeting, but for the most part his reaction was to tell JB to go to hell in a matter-of-fact manner using the F-word.

I quickly learned that the greeting was part of their relationship, and as such, it was a grand example of "permitted disrespect," the defining essence of a joking relationship (Radcliffe-Brown 1940). White Mike allowed JB to disrespect him in an aggressive and playful manner, a common occurrence among good friends. Mike, however, did not extend this allowance to everyone. Most of the Mexican patrons called him "White Mike," but the remarks about odor and incest only came from JB. Only twice did I hear two other

Mexican patrons greet White Mike in the same manner as JB. One was Leo and the other was Mr. Charlie, the octogenarian. Leo used the phrase during a domino game, but Mike ignored it, and I never heard Leo refer to White Mike in this manner again. Mr. Charlie, on the other hand, brought up the greeting regularly in a deliberately oblique and humorous tone. Its playfulness meant that Mr. Charlie was deliberately ridiculing Mike, albeit in a joking manner. These comments never failed to bring smiles and chuckles to the patrons who were present, and this, of course, was Mr. Charlie's intent. One afternoon, JB, Mr. Charlie, Gene, and I were playing dominoes. Mike was sitting at the bar drinking a beer and watching the game. We were the only patrons in the bar and Mike the only white patron.

> "JB what you think of ole White Mike?" Mr. Charlie asks. "Don't give me any of your shit today ole man," Mike responds, "I'm not in the mood." "I'm not trying to give you anything," Mr. Charlie answers in a congenial fashion. "I like you. If there is anybody in here that I like it's you. I don't care what JB says about you, you know, calling you stinky and smelly and all that stuff. I don't do that, I don't call you stinky and smelly, I like you." White Mike does not respond.

Other times Mr. Charlie called White Mike stinky or smelly and feigned a slip of the tongue. One afternoon, Mr. Charlie had been trying to lure him into a domino game. Mr. Charlie was sitting at the domino table and White Mike was at the bar with several other patrons. Again, Mike was the only white patron.

> "Hey, smelly I mean White Mike are you going to play?" "Fuck you Mr. Charlie," Mike tells him. Mr. Charlie laughs. "I didn't mean to call you smelly," he replies while laughing, "it's just that I hear JB say all that stuff about goat smelling and all that and sometimes I forget." He laughs again. The other patrons are smiling and chuckling.

On one occasion, White Mike revealed that JB received the phrase from him. The context was again a domino game. White Mike, Mr. Charlie, and I were playing and JB joined us. JB's entry into the game changed the dynamics. White Mike was now intent on stopping JB and tried to block his every move. After a few plays JB realized this and he engaged Mike. At the end of the exchange, White Mike called JB partner, a term that both he and JB often used that referenced their close friendship.

> "I know what you're trying to do, you goat smeller," JB tells White Mike. Mr. Charlie laughs. "Did you hear that?" Mr. Charlie asks me. "Did you ever hear anyone call some else a goat smeller?" He laughs again. "That shit doesn't bother me ole man," White Mike says. "I taught him that and he turned it on me and has been calling me that ever since. Didn't I teach you that JB?" "White boys haven't taught me shit," JB says slamming down a domino, "especially a goat-smelling motherfucker like you." We laugh. "Fuck you, partner," White Mike responds in a congenial fashion.

White Mike did indeed bring the phrase "goat-smelling motherfucker" to the bar. JB relayed that in White Mike's early years of patronage he used the term frequently to refer to both the Mexican and white patrons. Thus, the phrase "goat-smelling motherfucker" had been part of the bar's vernacular for nineteen years, the length of time Mike had been a patron. At some point JB appropriated the phrase and used it to address Mike while prefacing the phrase with "White Mike" and it was a complete appropriation. Only twice during the study did White Mike utter the expression, and both times to illustrate irritation at its usage (see below).

Sometimes in seeking a favor, JB softened his approach. Once, Mike volunteered to get some ice for JB, and JB's gentle tone of acceptance indicated supplication, but only for purposes of receiving the favor. It was early afternoon and Mike and Harvey were sitting at the bar watching us play dominoes. JB looked at his watch.

> "Damn it, I have to get some ice," he says. "You don't have any ice?" White Mike asks. "No," JB answers, "I was going to get some, but I got tied up with that damn roof." "Give me the keys and I'll go get your damn ice," Mike says. "Would you do that for me partner?" JB asks in a very friendly

manner. "Listen to this," Harvey says, "it used to be you goat-smelling motherfucker but now it's partner." "Well he's still that," JB responds, "but right now he's my partner." We laugh. "Fuck you JB," White Mike says as he walks out to get the ice.

To elaborate, the joking relationship between JB and White Mike illustrated a special bond. Mike accepted JB's playful aggression and did not object to JB's manner of addressing him because he viewed JB as a close friend. Close friendships involve a positive feeling towards another. It is one in which those involved have an emotional attachment. Those involved in such friendships have special license to say things about each other that others cannot say. Close friends explicitly or tacitly give and receive permission to disrespect each other in a playful manner. As mentioned, this defines a joking relationship and described JB's and White Mike's friendship. JB was the only Mexican in the bar who used the entire phrase "goat-smelling motherfucker" in addressing Mike. Not once did I hear another Mexican patron use the term beyond the two examples already cited, and White Mike did not correct either Leo or Mr. Charlie. Strangers and casual acquaintances, and perhaps even some close friends, could not address each other in this manner without causing conflict, but obviously, this did not describe JB and White Mike's symbiotic relationship. White Mike was the person whom JB relied upon for repairs to his bar. He worked on the bar's air conditioner and cooler and dealt with the plumbing and electrical issues numerous times. When someone burglarized the bar by breaking through the cinder blocks in the back, the first person JB called was White Mike, who closed the hole by welding and covering it with a large steel plate. White Mike charged JB for his services, but it was usually at a discounted rate and it always included some trading for beer. White Mike's minor repairs were always for beer. JB also sold him cases of beer at wholesale prices and gave him complete run of the bar, including keys to the place. If White Mike drove by in the early afternoon and patrons were outside waiting for JB to arrive, he would stop and open the bar and leave saying, "Tell JB I let you in." He also tended the bar when JB left to take care of errands. Even when JB was present, White Mike at times would sit behind the bar waiting on customers and handling the cash register and stocking beer in the cooler. When he was on his way to the bar, he would often call and ask if JB wanted something to eat. White Mike visited the bar daily and he and JB spoke regularly on the phone. Most of the calls were of the "just check-ing in" variety. These ongoing interactions illustrated mutual likability and trust, and regarding JB's greeting, an unstated understanding that it was said in jest and not to be taken personally. This was why Mike offered only mild resistance to the greeting by casually telling JB to go to hell by using the F-word.

Saving Face

Mike did not attempt to restrict the use of his nickname, White Mike, among the Mexican patrons, but on several occasions, he made it obvious he did not like for the white patrons to use it when addressing him. One afternoon a small group of whites was on the deck. I was the only Mexican present. Mike asked Tina if she had stored his phone number in her new cell phone.

"Let's see . . . White Mike . . ." Tina says scrolling down her list of stored names. "Damn," Mike responds in an irritated tone, "even white people call me White Mike!" Everyone laughs. "It's true, I can't get away from it. There used to be a couple of Meskin Mikes in here, but they don't come around anymore and haven't for a long time, but everybody here still calls me White Mike," he says in an exasperated manner.

During another gathering on the deck, one of Mike's white coworkers called him White Mike in a teasing manner and Mike quickly and firmly responded. "Hey," he said, "I don't play that shit with everyone." The co-worker looked down and did not respond. On another occasion as Mike was preparing to leave and bring his wife back to the bar, he asked the small group of Mexican patrons with whom he had been conversing not to call him White Mike in her presence. "Why not?" someone asked. "Because she may not understand," he responded. Mike also showed awareness of how entrenched his nickname was in the bar and the racial message it sent. One evening as I approached John, one of the Mexican patrons, and White Mike at the bar, John mentioned the Houston Rodeo and its Hispanic and African American Heritage Days. I did not hear what Mike said, but I deduced it was negative because John told him, "Damn, why does everything have to be racial?" "Because it's a fact of life," Mike responded. "Hell, everybody in here calls me White Mike, how much more racial do you want to get?"

White Mike displayed a sensitivity and defensiveness about his nickname with the white patrons that he did not express in his relationship with JB and the other Mexican patrons, and I speculate that it may have been because of Mexican-white relations in the broader society where whites have more prestige and status relative to Mexicans. Mexicans were not supposed to ridicule whites, especially to their face. Whites ridiculing Mexicans has been the historical norm, but in the bar the roles were reversed. Mike may have felt that to allow other whites to call him by his nickname was to be perceived as acquiescing to the Mexican patrons, a minority group perceived by some whites as inferior. Some evidence existed for this reasoning. One afternoon Mike's white supervisor walked into the bar with three of Mike's white coworkers. Mike was not present. The supervisor had previously patronized the bar, but it was the first time for the others. Upon entering the bar, the supervisor introduced the men to JB and some of the patrons and said, "This is Mike's hangout and everyone here calls him White Mike." The coworkers laughed. Whether they said anything about Mike's nickname at their worksite is, of course, unknown, but perhaps this is what Mike feared. He may not have wanted the nickname taken to his work for fear of ridicule and being perceived as compliant by not objecting to its use by the Mexican patrons. Mike's efforts to restrict its usage among the white patrons were an example of "face work," meaning an effort to maintain respect and an attempt to avoid embarrassment (Goffman 1955). Avoiding embarrassment is one of the strongest motivations influencing social interaction, especially avoiding its extreme form, humiliation. Everyone intuitively saves face in their day-to-day interactions. This becomes obvious when face is threatened. This explains why Mike did not want his nickname used in front of his wife. To expose himself to ridicule because of his race would have called his manhood and self-respect into question, and what man wants that to happen with his wife present?

To reiterate, racial humor was an integral part of the Mexican-white relationship in the bar. It was how the Mexican and white patrons defined and discussed the racial aspects of their relationship. Yet, the humor was not implicitly devoid of seriousness. It reflected aggression because of the racial belittling. It was allowed, however, because the humor implied that the patrons were just playing racial roles. Thus, the humor displayed a dual function (Stephenson 1951). On the one hand, it reflected conflict and strain in the Mexican-white relationship and the challenges to white hegemony in the broader society. On the other hand, it functioned as a safety valve because the physical and emotional tensions involved found release and were controlled through laughter. This was important. As stated, group laughter was an expression of collective pleasure, a feel-good emotion that everyone, performers and audience alike, shared, and the more a group laughed together, the greater the bond. The laughter also reflected consensus, for without a common understanding of Mexican-white relations the joking and teasing would not have been funny. People do not laugh at things they do not understand, but the patrons knew the reality of Mexican-white relations in the world outside of JB's and the inversion in the bar made fodder for laughter and comment.

CHAPTER THREE

White Patrons Push Back

Two differences were noted when the white patrons used microaggressions to criticize the Mexican patrons; they were less frequent and much milder. Not once did any of the white patrons use brown as an adjective, as in "brown boy" or "you brown ass," or use "boy" as a stand-alone descriptor. They used the slur Meskin, but the Mexican patrons' use of the term and its relative lack of sting as a derogatory term allowed them to do so. There were instances when the white patrons made forceful attacks, but again, on balance the microaggressions they leveled at the Mexican patrons were much less critical in tone. Thus, they were practicing a form of political correctness because the white patrons were fewer in numbers relative to the Mexican patrons and the bar was a Mexican bar located in a Mexican barrio. Given this environment, it is doubtful that the Mexican patrons would have tolerated equal treatment in terms of the content of the white patrons' racial attacks. It may also be reflecting the changing norms in society where whites making negative comments about minorities are less tolerated than in the past, especially in their presence.

Knives

One afternoon a group of patrons was playing dominoes. Manuel was the only white patron in the game and in the bar. A small group of Mexican patrons were standing at the bar watching the game and listening to their conversations.

> "Did you read the story in today's paper on which group is suffering the most causalities in Iraq?" Leo asks. "We are," Phil replies. "We are dying in greater proportions compared to our numbers in the military." "I'm not surprised," Johnny chimes in, "it's always been that way, Vietnam, Korea, World War II, hell we have the most medals." "It's because we are not scared," JB says. "No, it's because Mexicans are trying to fight with knives," Manuel says in a normal tone of voice with a smile on his face. Everyone chuckles. "Y'all should know that," he says.

Manuel drew upon the stereotype of Mexican males always carrying and using knives in fights to explain why Mexicans have always died in greater numbers fighting the country's wars (Nericcio 2007). Mexicans' proclivity for knives apparently stems from their Aztec Indian heritage and their use of knives during religious ceremonies to kill those who were used as victims for sacrifice (Graulich 2000). Most of the soldiers fighting America's wars, of course, fought with guns. Mexicans, however, according to Manuel, used knives as was their tradition and thus died in greater numbers. Everyone laughed because of their familiarity with the stereotype. There was no animosity in Manuel's tone, only the intent to be humorous by relying upon a shared stereotype. As such, it was a gentle tease.

Another comment that involved the knives stereotype was said in a non-humorous, tentative, and anxious tone by Harvey. Efren asked Harvey how long he had been coming to JB's. "Twenty-eight years," Harvey replied, and he proceeded with a story of how Tony, his Mexican boss, brought him to the bar. It was his first ever encounter with Mexicans and he liked it and returned several times with Tony, but after a few more visits he wanted to come alone.

"So, you know one day I wanted to come by myself, but I was a bit hesitant. I didn't know how, you know, how I would be received because I'm white and you know, Meskins carry knives" (*laughs nervously*) "but I told myself, so be it, and decided to come anyway, and when I walked in JB said in a loud voice, "Harvey, where in the hell have you been?" and I knew right then everything was going to be alright."

Harvey did not know much about Meskins, but what he knew was stereotypical, they carried knives, and this made him hesitant perhaps because he feared they might not like whites and possibly stab him. His fears caused trepidation but "so be it," he came anyway. He wanted to hang out with the Mexicans regardless of any danger to his life. His concerns were immediately relieved when JB greeted him. Harvey told several variations of the same story and always mentioned his fretting over how everyone would react because of his whiteness, but this was the first time he mentioned knives. His tentative manner in saying the words "Meskins carried knives" indicated he knew it was a negative image and did not wish to offend, but he nevertheless said it, and no one questioned him. Things turned out well for Harvey. He had been a patron for twenty-eight years and had never been stabbed. He did, however, engage in strident exchanges with Efren, as illustrated below.

Drunkards

Another Mexican stereotype surfaced in a conversation about the Vaqueros' impending trail ride from San Antonio to Houston. It had been a topic for several days because several patrons were participating. The weather was going to be cold during the two-week ride. In the evenings, when the Vaqueros camped out for the night, there was usually a fiesta. In a matter-of-fact tone, White Mike said Meskins used the trail ride as just another excuse to get drunk, and he laughed. He implied drunkenness was normal Mexican behavior. Research has shown that Mexican males consume less than white males but tend to binge or fiesta drink when drinking in a group, and this, of course, was the circumstance defining the trail ride (Gonzalez et al. 2015). Fiesta drinking was also common in JB's, and White Mike drank as much as any of the Mexican patrons, but he did not find camping out on a cold night after a day of riding a horse or in a wagon and getting drunk as ideal. He believed it was just another excuse for Mexicans to get intoxicated. Rather, he preferred being in the woods hunting deer on a cold morning and getting drunk at night. He seemed to ignore that this was the same behavior as the Vaqueros when they camped out at night. Mike and I were standing at the bar talking when he brought up the Vaquero trail riders.

"The trail riders are leaving tonight, and tomorrow my wife and I are going to ride by those cold bastards and wave hello," he says laughing. "Will you be on the trail ride?" I ask. "Hell no, my wife and I rented a hotel room for $160 a night on the River Walk so we will be in San Antonio, but I wouldn't spend my money on that damn trail ride anyway. Hell, it's just another reason for Meskins to get drunk," he says laughing, "you know how Meskins are." He takes a drink of his beer and continues, "But you know I will spend two or three thousand a year going deer hunting in the cold, so I guess it's all about what appeals to you. I'm going to the deer lease in a couple of weeks to put out some feed, but hell no, you won't catch me on any damn trail ride and getting drunk with the Meskins. Hell, I'll drink beer and get drunk after I hunt deer."

Incest

Another matter-of-fact racial critique involved a mild "gotcha" moment. The Mexican patrons at times teased the white patrons, especially those with rural backgrounds, about their alleged inclination towards incest as part of white trailer-trash culture. One afternoon Mike got the opportunity to return the charge by implying that Mexicans "inbreed" more than whites. It was early afternoon, and JB, White Mike, and I were the only patrons in the bar. JB began telling us about a funeral he had attended earlier in the day. He said he discovered new relatives and gave a complicated description of how their kinship wove through his extended family and eventually to him.

> "Man, I keep finding out I'm kin to just about everyone. Everywhere I go I find a new relative, it happens all the time, I mean all the time." "And you keep saying white people are always inbreeding," Mike says, "hell it's Meskins who are doing the inbreeding. Look at all the kids you have. Hell, all of you are somehow kinfolk, it's Meskins who are the inbreeders." JB does not respond.

The racial exchange was conducted in a normal tone of voice. White Mike scored a racial point in a matter-of-fact manner when he described what he thought was the ordinary nature of sexual behavior among Meskins. All Meskins married "kinfolk" and hence all were related. Meskins were "the inbreeders." The traditional high birth rates among Mexican women was his evidence.

Ripping Off White People

Occasionally Jerry, the small-business owner, also gained the upper hand in the racial exchanges in which he was involved. One afternoon several patrons were sitting in a circle on the deck talking about how to make money, and during the discussion, Kid alleged that Jerry exploited Mexicans. Jerry was the only white patron present.

> "I know how to hustle," Kid says leaning forward, "because of my dad taught me how. He was always hustling a living for us and I learned from him, so I know I won't starve if I ever lose my job." "Hell, I have to hustle every day," Johnny says, "because if I don't complete my route I'll get fired. Delivering mail requires hustling every day." "You must hustle if you want to make it," Jerry interjects, "especially if you own your own business like I do, I really have to hustle." "Yeah, we know how Mexicans are helping you make a living," Kid quickly responds, "but are you helping them? How

many Mexicans did you help today?" Everyone laughs. "Well they do help me make a living, but I pay them. I'm working on Victor's house right now, his wife has a lot of things she wants done," Jerry responds. "That's my point," Kid says in animated fashion, "first you hire my people to work for you and don't pay them anything and then you work on my people's houses and charge them high prices. I don't do that; I don't take advantage of my people. I know how to make honest money." "Yeah you sure do," Jerry responds in a sarcastic tone. "You know," he says to everyone, "one time Kid sold me a bottle of cologne for $35 and later I read on the bottom of the bottle that it was a sample and not for resale and then I see the same bottle at the mall selling for $8." Everyone laughs. "And to top it off," Jerry continues, "the stuff smelled so bad not even my dog would come around me when I wore that shit." The laughter continues. "Yeah, but I don't rip my people off," Kid says while grinning. "You don't have to rip off 'my people,'" Jerry responds in a loud, sarcastic tone, "because you're ripping off white people like me, you're ripping us off." Everyone laughs again. "Now, come on Jerry, you know that cologne helped you get women," Kid says with a big grin on his face. "It helped me get shit," Jerry responds again in a louder voice. "I tell you not even my dog would come around me it smelled so bad." Everyone continues laughing.

When Kid said he did not exploit "my people" the charge was quickly turned against him. Kid did not have to exploit Mexicans, Jerry retorted, because he had whites like him to exploit. If whites did not exist, Jerry implied "my people" would be Kid's target. In other words, whites were stand-ins for Kid's shady actions. Jerry turned Kid's accusations of exploitation against him and gained laughter and the last word.

Green Go

Although Jerry mimicked minorities in his role-playing during the white quota exchanges, on occasion, his race-related comments took a serious tone and he pushed back, as minorities do in the real world. This was evident in the following scenario because he was not in the conversation but rather was part of the audience and sitting several stools away from a small group at the bar. Mr. Jim and Jerry were the only white patrons present. The exchange began when Mr. Jim asked JB if he could use his cell phone. JB handed him the phone.

> "I need to call my *abogado* [lawyer]," Mr. Jim says, showing off one of his few words of Spanish. He dials a number and then stares at the phone trying to figure out how to send it. JB stands beside him watching, and after a few moments, he says, "The red button means stop and the green button means go. I learned that as a kid, green go, green go." Everyone laughs but Jerry does not. "Fuck you, JB," he says from the other end of the bar in a defensive tone.

JB garnered laugher with his intentional homonym word play for gringo, a well-known derogatory term used by Mexicans to describe whites (Allen 1983; Paredes 1961). As a white person, Jerry obviously felt the need to defend Mr. Jim, and by inference, all white people. Despite the teasing context, Jerry did not find JB's clever remarks amusing. His pushback stood out because he was several feet away from the small group and it was said loud enough for everyone to hear. Indeed, his counterattack consisted of only three words, "Fuck you, JB," said in a direct and unsmiling manner. JB and the others ignored the remark and Mr. Jim placed his call.

Where's My Change

As mentioned, White Mike and JB had a very cordial relationship. It was obvious that they liked each other and had a true friendship. Yet as in all social relationships, there were instances of strain that at times led to a defensive posture from both. One Saturday afternoon JB deliberately and playfully forgot to give Mike his change, thereby making Mike feel unappreciated. It was surprising to see Mike respond in an irritated manner because it was obvious that JB was teasing. Deliberately keeping his change would have been out of character for JB, and Mike's failure to realize this was surprising. The presence of other patrons and their laughter may have induced him to react aggressively. He had to save face and JB playfully helped him, but it was interesting to see White Mike's reaction considering other teasing episodes involving JB. It was unanticipated because it concerned what seemed like a minor issue. It occurred when several patrons were on the deck drinking beer and eating barbecue. Mike was sitting at one of the picnic tables. JB walked out of the bar towards the deck carrying a bucket of beer. He handed the bucket to Mike, who in turn handed some money to JB, who then turned and began to walk away.

> "Where's my goddamn change?" Mike asks in an irritated tone. "I didn't give it to you?" JB asks turning around. "You know damn well you didn't," Mike says, holding out his hand. "Well let's just say it's your storage fee for leaving your motorbike here overnight," JB says laughing. "The hell it is," Mike quickly responds in a defensive manner, "the next time you have a leak in the cooler I'll just let the motherfucker leak!" "Well, in that case I had better give your change because I need my white labor," JB says laughing and handing Mike his change. "Your damn cheap white labor," Mike responds, still sounding irritated. "That too," JB says while grinning. Several of us laugh, but Mike does not.

Intermarriage

In the following exchange, neither JB nor White Mike laughed or gave any indication they were kidding. One late afternoon several patrons were on the deck listening to JB talk about four brothers who were his friends. White Mike and Jake were the only white patrons present.

> "Do they have any sisters?" someone asks. "One and she's married to a white boy," JB responds. "What the hell is wrong with that?" White Mike immediately asks in an aggressive tone. The patrons chuckle at his quick response. "Nothing," JB says, "I just mentioned she's married to a white

boy, that's all." "Yeah, but you made it sound like there was something wrong with it," White Mike quickly answers again. "Well, the brothers don't like him," JB responds. "But is it because he's white?" Mike persists. "Hell, I don't know and what if it is?" JB defiantly answers. There is a moment of silence before White Mike responds. "Shit," he says, "well let me tell you about this white friend of ours, and Jake you know who I'm talking about, he's married to this ole Meskin gal, and man she is one mean motherfucker, isn't that right Jake?" "Oh yeah," Jake quickly responds, "I know exactly who you are talking about and she is one mean bitch." "She's so goddamn mean," White Mike continues, "he's afraid to leave her because he's scared she'll kill his ass." No one responds, and the exchange ends in silence.

Was a Mexican marrying a white person wrong? White Mike believed that JB meant it was wrong because he described the sister of a friend as being married to a "white boy" in a manner that implied it was a bad thing to do. This threatened White Mike, as indicated by his quick response, defensive tone, and persistence in seeking an affirmation or denial. He wanted to know if whiteness was the issue. What he received, however, was a challenge if indeed it was an issue. White Mike paused for a moment and did not pursue the challenge. Rather he countered with a negative story about a mean Mexican woman to rival the negative image of whiteness implied by JB. It was a competing statement that messaged, "If white males are bad marriage partners, so are Mexican women." He called upon Jake, his white friend, for support, and he willingly complied on cue as if it was all deliberately coordinated. The exchange ended with the issue of whether Mexican-white marriages were a bad thing unresolved. For the record, intermarriage rates between Mexicans and whites increase with each new generation and approach 40 percent by the third generation, illustrating that a significant number of Mexicans and whites do not seem to think it is a bad idea (Duncan and Trejo 2011; Rosenfeld 2002). Nevertheless, the comments revealed a strained moment between JB and White Mike. Clearly White Mike perceived JB's comments as a putdown of whites and he took immediate offense. The audience chuckled at the beginning of White Mike and JB's retorts, but was silent by the time it ended because everyone became aware of the changed tenor of the exchange.

Efren and the White Patrons

Efren was not only a patron, he was also JB's part-time bartender and close friend. He tended the bar in the evenings and on the weekends and often worked during the day when JB had errands to run. Efren and JB conversed a great deal in Spanish and referred to each other as *compadre*, a term that signaled a special and close friendship. At times JB emphasized affection by addressing Efren as *mi compadre favorito* or *mi compadre lindo*, "my favorite friend" or "my cute friend." Efren was a widower and had been a patron of the bar for only six years, but had lived in Second Ward with his wife and family for over thirty years and had kinship ties with some of the patrons. He also knew some of the patrons before he started coming to the bar. Efren and Leo, for example, were both teamsters and had been friends for more than twenty years. When Leo cooked at the bar, Efren helped, and at times Efren cooked by himself.

Several aspects about Efren's personality were immediately noted. He consistently expressed pride in his Mexican heritage. When the Mexican patrons called him a wetback because of his birth in Mexico, he would respond in a pugnacious manner, "You're damn right, I'm a damn proud Mexican." Efren also had a penchant for uttering profanities. He had a kind, grandfatherly look and his profanity did not fit the perception. Yet Efren always seemed to be engaged in dispute performances (Pagliai 2010) telling some patron "fuck you" or calling someone a "motherfucker" or telling someone "don't fuck with me." Efren was also the recipient of excessive and aggressive teasing, and his tormentors included both the Mexican and white patrons. He was told he was slow, shouldn't be playing dominoes when he ought to be tending bar, failed to buy some item needed for cooking, didn't start the fire on the grill, forgot to put ice in the beer cooler, failed to clean the restroom, opened late, cursed, smoked and drank too much, liked fat women, and on and on. Efren did not take the teasing passively.

He responded as forcibly as he received and usually with more intensity. He displayed hostility towards both the Mexican and white patrons, but in his insults of the white patrons he drew sharp racial distinctions with his use of "white" as adjective to convey to his targets that they were more despicable because of their race.

One evening a group of patrons was standing at the bar. Harvey and Jerry were the only white patrons present. Benny inquired about a shuffleboard tournament being held at another bar. This led to Efren forcibly claiming superiority over "your people" in shuffleboard. Surprisingly, Jerry did not initially grasp Efren's racial distinction. He thought "your people" referred to people born outside of the United States, but his reasoning why was not clear.

"Efren, what time does the tournament start?" Benny asks. "Six-thirty," Efren responds. "What tournament?" Harvey asks. "The shuffleboard tournament," Benny responds. "Where?" Harvey asks, "at Beamers?" "Yeah," Efren answers, and "you are looking at the champion." "You're the champion of the shuffleboard tournament?" Harvey asks somewhat surprised. "You're damn right and I beat your people," Efren responds belligerently. "My people?" Harvey asks. "You're damn right," Efren answers, "your people can't play worth a shit." "Who is your people?" Jerry asks. "Your goddamn people," Efren responds with force. "You see there are my people and there are your people, and your goddamn white people lost." "Hell, I don't know why you say your people," Jerry responds, "I don't have a purple card like you do. I was born here." We laugh. "It's not a purple card, it's a green card," someone says. Everyone laughs. "Well, Efren has had his so long that it has turned purple," Jerry says as the laughter continues.

One afternoon several people were on the deck teasing Efren about his behavior at the previous day's fundraiser for the Vaqueros. This led to a litany of Efren's sins. It began when someone pointed out that Efren was giving plates of food away to the women during the barbecue because he was "trying to get some." Kid said that Efren failed to get enough ice and did not stay behind the bar. JB followed with a story about Efren "fucking up" some sheet rock. Harvey then started criticizing Efren for going through Leo's briefcase. Throughout the criticisms, Efren was listening with his head on the table, but when Harvey began to speak, he looked up as Harvey went on and on about going through Leo's briefcase.

> "What the hell is wrong with you?" Harvey asks emphatically. "You don't go through a man's briefcase, that's like going through his wallet. You should know better, what the hell is wrong with you?" "You white son of a bitch," Efren responds in an angry tone, "were you there? Do you know what happened? You stupid white ass, you don't know a damn thing." Efren stares at Harvey for a moment, picks up the newspaper, and pretends that he is reading. It is obvious that he is angry. The teasing subsides.

In the next scenario, Harvey was persistent in wanting to know who was going to work the bar when Efren went to Las Vegas. He asked Efren several times but did not receive an answer. Harvey pushed the issue and kept asking until Efren finally responded with an insult. He belittled Harvey's origins in Louisiana, using "white" as an adjective to imply that it was part of the reason that Harvey was among the lower dregs of the Caucasian race in Louisiana. JB came to Harvey's defense by asking Efren, "What are you?" and Efren countered with a strong assertion of his racial affiliation. Throughout, both Harvey and Efren were trying to gain dominance by raising their voices. Their performances created smiles and laughter among the audience, but neither Harvey nor Efren were kidding. They were serious. The drama took a break when Efren abruptly stopped and went to the restroom and the audience began to relax. They were reengaged when Efren returned and won the exchange through a clever and deceptive interpretation of a Spanish-language song that started playing on the jukebox. He secured dominance by attacking not only Harvey's whiteness but other personal characteristics as well, a tactic common among highly aggressive personalities (Infante et al. 1992).

> "When are you going to Las Vegas?" Harvey asks Efren. Efren ignores Harvey, but Harvey pushes the issue and asks several more times. Each

time Efren ignores the question. "Don't fuck with me fat boy," Efren finally responds in a forceful manner. "I'm not fucking with you. I just want to know when you're leaving town and who is going to work the place. Do you know when he is going?" Harvey asks JB. Efren stares at Harvey and says, "It's none of your business, you fucking coon ass." "And what are you?" JB asks Efren. "And do you know what a coon ass is?" Harvey asks. "You want to know what I am?" Efren says to JB, "I'm a Mexican and damn proud of it!" "And what's a coon ass?" Harvey asks again, "and don't let your mouth overload your ass." We chuckle. "Let me rephrase that," JB says, "don't let your crocodile mouth overload your hummingbird ass." Everyone laughs. Harvey stands and says in a loud voice "A coon ass is the asshole of a coon and it looks like this," and he makes a small round circle with his thumb and forefinger. "No, no, a coon ass is a white, fat motherfucker like you," Efren answers just as loudly. The patrons laugh. Efren and Harvey begin repeating their assertions at the same time, raising their voices trying to outshout each other, with Efren emphasizing white motherfucker and Harvey stressing coon ass. It goes on for several seconds, getting louder each time. "Fuck you," Efren suddenly says and heads towards the restroom. The heightened atmosphere begins to lessen, and the patrons return to their beer and conversations. After a few minutes Efren reappears, walks to the bar, and stands to the right of Harvey, who is sitting a few stools away. A song in Spanish comes on the jukebox and Harvey starts swaying back and forth and says to no one in particular, "You know when I first started coming in here I'd hear that song and I fell in love with it and I used to give JB some money and tell him to play it. I don't understand what it says but I sure love the melody." "You don't know what it's about?" Efren asks in a loud voice. Harvey shakes his head no. "It's about a white fat-ass coon boy like you," Efren says. Everyone bursts out laughing. "Fuck you," Harvey says, but his retort is drowned out by the laughter.

Provoked

At times, the patrons deliberately teased Efren with the intent to provoke and antagonize him because they knew that he would respond in an aggressive tone. As such, these episodes were grand examples of stimulus and response for the sole purpose of entertainment. One evening several of us were standing at the bar talking. Efren was bartending and listening. Manuel was the only white patron present. The deliberate teasing of Efren began when Leo asked for service.

> "Give us a bucket, Efren bin Laden, and hurry," Leo says. Everyone laughs. "Don't be fucking with me, I'm not in the mood," Efren responds as he starts to prepare the bucket. Manuel pokes me gently in the ribs, winks, and then says out loud, "You mean ole Efren has been slowing down on the job?" "Don't you fuck with me either you old white fucker," Efren quickly responds in a defiant tone, "fuck you." Everyone at the bar smiles knowingly. Manuel, smiling, looks at me, winks again, and takes a sip of his drink.

Manuel received the response he sought, and on cue, Efren fulfilled his expectation. His goal was to needle Efren and get him to aggressively respond for the audience's entertainment, and he succeeded. Everyone saw what Manuel was up to. His first wink conveyed that he was going to deliberately tease to provoke Efren, and his second wink indicated success. Manuel obviously enjoyed his orchestration.

Exploitation

Manuel had extensive involvement with Mexicans in his personal life as well as in his business dealings. Most of his female companions throughout his adult life were Mexicans. He was once married to a Mexican woman and had a daughter from the marriage whom he described as "fully bi-lingo." He once told me, "Mexican women are the best. They appreciate things.

They are not like high-dollar white women who have to go to fancy places." Manuel was now married to a woman from Honduras whom he described as "almost like a Mexican." His wife did not speak English and Manuel did not speak Spanish. When I asked how they communicated, he laughed and said, "We deal with it and things work out." For more than twenty years Manuel owned Players, a popular Mexican bar on the north side of Houston. When he began visiting JB's, he knew most of the Mexican patrons because they used to frequent his bar. Manuel was retired but continued to lease 8 Liners, pool tables, and jukeboxes, and said he only did business with Mexican bars because they were the most trustworthy and lucrative.

One afternoon Manuel's involvement with Mexicans became a cause for laughter. It included a double entendre using the F-word. There were a dozen patrons present and Manuel was the only white patron. Someone said that the Houston Texans were playing their first game in their new stadium next Sunday and asked if anyone was going. Big Daddy said that he hoped the people who attended the football game enjoyed "being screwed" because they were the ones who were going to pay for the stadium. This started Manuel on one of his favorite harangues, the high cost of attending professional sporting events and millionaire African American players. Manuel was addressing his remarks to the whole group, but Efren seemed to take offense. The exchanges were loud because Manuel was sitting at the domino table and most of the other patrons were at the bar a few feet away. Efren was behind the bar and his comments were the loudest.

"That's what I'm talking about," Manuel says, "poor people of all kinds, Mexicans, niggers, and whites, are being ripped off because they can't afford to go to the games. They have priced the poor people and their kids out and that's why I won't attend any professional games, basketball, football, baseball, none of them. Fuck-em!" "If you care so damn much for the poor," Efren tells Manuel from behind the bar in a loud voice, "why don't you do something about it?" "What do you want me to do?" Manuel quickly replies, "buy tickets for 50 million kids? I don't have that kind of money, but if I wanted to go to the games, I could afford the best tickets in the house, but I'm not going to give them a shadow of a dime. Tell me, do you think Duck can afford to take his wife and three kids to the ballpark on his salary? Hell, how many Mexicans can afford to take their kids to games, and for what, to watch a bunch of goddamn millionaire niggers run up and down the field? Not me, fuck-em!" "If you're so damn worried about the poor Mexicans," Efren persists, "why don't you take some to the games? You don't give a damn about poor Mexicans, you're just a damn liar!" "I don't lie," Manuel responds forcibly. "Oh yes you do," Efren quickly retorts, "it's just like you saying you never go out to the deck." "I don't," Manuel replies, "I never go out there." "That's a goddamn white lie!" Efren says. We laugh lightly at the double meaning of Efren's response. "Hey," Gilbert interjects, "I can personally vouch for Manuel because he has been fucking Mexicans for over forty years." "Ohhhh," the patrons howl loudly while laughing. Kid strokes his chin in a pondering fashion and repeats Gilbert's statement: "Manuel has been fucking Mexicans for over forty years, I'm going to have to think about that one."

Gilbert intended his use of the F-word to have a double meaning. It referred to Manuel's sexual relations with his ex-wife and other Mexican women while also implying that Manuel exploited Mexicans through his business dealings. Everyone laughed because of their familiarity with Manuel's history. Manuel's use of the N-word and Efren's tone in challenging Manuel indicated animosity. Manuel intensely disliked African Americans and was very pro-Mexican, but Efren appeared to resent Manuel's defense of poor Mexicans; yet it was not clear why he questioned Manuel's sincerity. Manuel had made a good living, loved to gamble in the casinos, bet on professional sports through the bookies, and always seemed to have several hundred dollars in his pocket. Perhaps these signals told Efren that Manuel was showing off. A white lie is one of small consequence, but within the context of the exchange, Efren's intent was to tell Manuel that as a liar he was more despicable because he was white, but it generated only mild laughter. Gilbert's clever entendre generated a much more hilarious reaction.

Efren and White Mike

Often Efren's use of the word "white" as an adjective occurred during heated exchanges while playing dominoes. One afternoon the profanity was heavy as the players criticized each other's plays. The exchanges between Efren and White Mike were particularly harsh, and in one instance, Mike pushed back to Efren's racial epithet with a threat. It began when they started arguing and accusing each other of playing the wrong domino. The argument went back and forth and ended with both White Mike and Efren yelling at each other.

"Fuck you, you white motherfucker," Efren yells at White Mike in a tone of finality. "Listen you old motherfucker, I'm getting tired of your shit; you better watch your goddamn mouth," Mike responds in a loud voice. Efren does not answer and the game proceeds in silence for a few minutes.

One afternoon White Mike used the term white to bring attention to his whiteness, but he conveyed a different meaning in comparison to how the Mexican patrons used the term. It occurred after a domino game and again involved Efren. He was the big winner and White Mike was one of the losers. After the game had ended, Efren began teasing Mike in an aggressive manner. Efren's intent was to irritate Mike for losing by "rubbing it in" and to boast about his winnings. Several patrons were in the bar. Mike was the only white patron and was sitting by himself at the domino table. Efren was sitting at the bar with a bucket of beer in front of him. He turned his stool and faced Mike. Note that White Mike introduced race when Geraldo involved himself in the give-and-take with Efren.

"I'm drinking this bucket off you," Efren says. White Mike does not respond. Efren repeats himself several times and emphasizes how much he is enjoying the beer. White Mike refuses to respond and Efren changes tactics. "You know, you sure can fuck up a game," he says. White Mike does not respond, and Efren repeats himself several times. "Fuck you, motherfucker, I didn't fuck up shit; I play the hand I get, motherfucker," White Mike suddenly responds in a loud voice. "Damn," Geraldo tells White Mike, "you have an attitude." "Fuck you too, you can kiss my white ass," White Mike tells Geraldo quick and loud. "Like I said, you have an attitude," Geraldo replies. The exchange ends.

White Mike's provoked hostility was obvious in its stridency and profanity. It consisted of twenty-four words, a quarter of which were profane. Efren did not respond to White Mike's provocation. He sat at the bar smiling, looking satisfied after having forced White Mike to respond to his ridicule. He had achieved his mission. He criticized White Mike to the point of anger by getting "under his skin." When Geraldo noted White Mike's "attitude," White Mike attacked him by telling him where to go and to "kiss my white ass." The image of a Mexican literally kissing that area of a white body associated with human waste was an insult, but Geraldo ignored the insult by using it as an example of White Mike's aggressive and negative mindset, that is, his "attitude."

At times Efren's aggressive responses were unexpected, perhaps because he could not always tell the difference between teasing and serious attacks. One afternoon Efren, Harvey, Leo, and I were on the deck. Efren was working a crossword puzzle and filling in the blanks with Harvey's assistance. Efren frequently worked crossword puzzles to test his knowledge of English. The tenor of their interactions up to the point of Efren's angry attack consisted of good-natured bantering over which words to use. They contested each other's suggestions in a friendly manner, and Harvey's tease of Efren about not being able to work a puzzle in either English or Spanish was said in the same good-natured style. Apparently, however, Efren did not perceive it as such, as evidenced by his unexpected angry response. Perhaps he felt especially attacked because Harvey included the Spanish language in his jibe. Efren, after all, consistently proclaimed his pride in being a Mexican, and his angry response may have been to protect his honor, a common reaction when an audience was present. Efren could not always tell when he was being teased because, I speculate, of his sensitivity over his knowledge of the English language, and this often led to his angry retorts (Felson 1978). The incident began when Efren asked Harvey for the meaning of a word. He rejected Harvey's suggestion, used another word, and complained when it did not fit.

> "I told you what the right word is, but you wouldn't listen," Harvey says. "He thought it was a Spanish word," Leo interjects. "Hell, he can't work a puzzle in either language," Harvey says. Efren quickly looks up and says in an angry tone, "Fuck you, you white motherfucker." Leo laughs while Efren and Harvey stare at each other for a second and then Efren resumes looking at the crossword puzzle.

I once asked JB why the Mexican and white patrons teased Efren so much. JB laughed and said that everyone liked Efren, and when he reacted to teasing, he did so deliberately in an exaggerated fashion. I agreed. Efren was a regular patron, an insider, JB's compadre and part-time bartender. When he was not present for a few days, the other patrons inquired about his whereabouts. When he became ill, they consistently inquired about his well-being. At times, it was obvious he feigned hostility, but it was hard to decipher his reactions because they tended to carry the same intensity whether joking or not. Everyone liked Efren, but he was also everyone's favorite punching bag, and when he pushed back, playfully or not, against the white patrons their race was one of his weapons.

Conclusions

The white patrons' "minority status" played a major role in their less vociferous racial attacks upon the Mexicans. They were a numerical minority with less power and prestige in the bar. Many times, there were only one or two white patrons in the bar, and even when more white patrons were present, they were usually small in number. Had their numbers been larger, perhaps there would have been more joking parity with the Mexican patrons, but given the bar's location and its clientele, perhaps not. It was doubtful the Mexican patrons would have tolerated "equal treatment" in terms of the frequency and content of the joking that was aimed in their direction. It was, after all, their bar.

Also probable was the change in public norms. Public expressions of racial prejudice were now taboo and there were sanctions against those who uttered them. It was no longer permissible for racial groups to disparage other racial groups in public, especially to their face, and the white population bore more of the burden of complying because of their historical and contemporary relations with other racial groups in the United States. Some whites pushed back, but most acquiesced to the new norm out of courtesy and support, or because of fear of saying something wrong and enduring consequences (Ely, Meyerson, and Davidson 2006). Hence, they exhibited a degree of caution and timidity. Even in a mixed racial setting like JB's, where race talk was ongoing, this new norm may explain why the white patrons did not engage in the same kind of aggressive racial teasing they experienced. There seemed to be an imaginary boundary they would not cross, even within the context of the racial joking norm that existed in the bar. At times, the Mexican patrons deliberately provoked the white patrons, and at times the white patron said negative things about Mexicans in a matter-of-fact manner, and both groups were defensive when attacked, but there was more caution among the white patrons.

An interaction with Tina, the only white female patron who patronized the bar on a regular basis, was illustrative. It occurred in a conversation about the high cost of health care. We were discussing an editorial that appeared in the *Houston Chronicle* about corruption in the health-care system in Hidalgo County, located on the U.S.-Mexico border in South Texas. Linda, a Mexican nurse, was listening. Tina was careful and deliberate in saying that she felt that Mexican immigrants were the reason for the corruption. It was clear she wanted to express her opinion, but also sought not to offend.

"Well ..." she says slowly ... "I don't want to be picking on any one group but, you know ... don't you think ...you know ... the people coming over from Mexico and ... uh ... using our health system ...you know ... might have something to do with it?" "It could," I reply, "but I have not heard or read anything—" "I have, and I've seen it," Linda interrupts without hesitation. "They do it all the time and it's part of the reason why our health costs are so high." Tina gives me a glance and says, "You know that's what I was trying to say."

Tina was initially cautious. She carefully framed her thoughts by prefacing her sentiments with a denial of wanting to pick on "any one group" and then haltingly and timidly proceeded to do so by soliciting my consideration with "don't you think . . ." She received cover from Linda, who immediately agreed that immigrants were the reason for high health costs, which she verified with "I've seen it." A Mexican nurse made it okay for Tina to express her sentiments because of her intersecting racial and occupational status. The trepidation initially expressed by Tina may also have reflected what inhibited the white male patrons when they engaged in race talk. If true it was an example of self-imposed political correctness, a notion they ridiculed (Ely, Meyerson, and Davidson 2006). They liked the Mexicans and the Mexicans liked them, but likability did not evaporate history and their respective racial consciousness. The nature of the race talk in the bar was a symbol of changing times in society where American-born and/or reared Mexicans were being more assertive in combating prejudice and discrimination.

CHAPTER FOUR

Meskins, Peppers, Being White, and Slurs

acial slurs are microaggressions that insult and disparage a group of people because of their race. They are found among all peoples of the world, especially in areas where different ethnic and racial groups reside. Such slurs go hand in hand with the social construction of race and are used as a justification for racial stratification. They are the language of conflict and function to draw racial boundaries, express prejudice, and justify discrimination (Allen 1983). They are verbal acts that wound and cause emotional and psychological pain, anger, and resentment (Hill 2008). Some argue that racial slurs are analogous to physical assaults that can provoke violent reactions (Matsuda et al. 1993).

Among the slurs used to describe Mexicans in Texas are "mongrel," "greaser," "spic," "pepper belly," "beaner," and "wetback" (Allen 1983; De Leon 1983). A mongrel is a mixed-breed dog considered less pure, and hence inferior. Whites used the term in the 1820s to refer to Mexicans because of their Indian-Spanish mix. "Greaser" has two possible origins. One is the swarthy and perceived oily complexion of Mexicans that allegedly made them look greasy. The second stems from the work that Mexicans performed for the railroads when they came to Texas. They greased the wheels of the trains as they pulled into the station by running alongside them with greased rags at the end of long sticks. As such, they were greasers (McWilliams and Meier 1990). "Spic" is believed to have originated from monolingual Spanish-speaking Mexicans who told whites, "no spika de English" (Flexner 1976). "Spic" was used to disparage Italians for the same reason when they began emigrating to the United States in the early 1900s. Peppers and beans are among the staples of the Mexican diet, and thus the slurs "pepper belly" and "beaner." The slur "wetback" stems from Mexicans swimming across the Rio Grande River to enter the United States, literally with a wet back. In the 1950s the U.S. government popularized the term when it initiated a Mexican deportation program officially called Operation Wetback (García 1980). In the bar, the Mexican patrons used the slur "wetback" to refer to people from Mexico. Efren was the only patron in the bar who was born in Mexico, and often during teasing exchanges was called a wetback. He frequently returned the slur and called Mexico "that wetback country." Efren and Mr. Charlie repeatedly called each other wetback. Racial slurs vary in intensity. Beaner, for example, is not as negative as greaser, wetback, or spic—the three Mexican slurs most often cited in dictionaries of slang (Green 1998; Spears 2001, 2006). Often soft slurs can easily acquire more harshness depending upon context.

The concern here is with the slur "Meskin," the mangling of the noun Mexican. When I was growing up in Houston, the phrases "damn Meskin" and "dirty Meskins" were applied to me and the broader Mexican community. Thus, I was surprised that both the Mexican and white patrons used the term and that it was not a point of contention given their other racial exchanges. Their use, however, differed. The Mexican patrons used the term in an affectionate in-group sense, while the white patrons used it with impunity as a common, everyday descriptor and the Mexican patrons did not complain or retaliate.

"Meskin" does not appear in some well-known dictionaries of slang (e.g., Green 1998; Spears 2001, 2006) indicating it was not in wide circulation. The website *Urban Dictionary* states it is a derogatory term unique to South

Texas and is similar in connotation to the N-word but not as offensive ("Meskin," 2011). Another source stated it may or may not be contemptuous and pointed out it was a quicker way of saying Mexican and could be a colloquialism sometimes spelled *Mescan* (Atwood 1962). Internet research revealed 239 people in the United States with the last name Meskin, including thirty eight whose ethnicity was listed as Hispanic. It could not be determined if any of the Hispanics were of Mexican heritage (American Surnames n.d.). These findings suggest why "Meskin" may not be offensive, but it is possible that in Texas, where the term originated, it was more likely to be considered a slur, as the following scenario indicated. One afternoon, Rubio, one of JB's longtime friends, told a story about Abel, a patron of a club that Rubio once owned. Abel was known to many of JB's patrons. There were several patrons on the deck listening.

> "Abel used to hang around my club all the time. One night this Anglo cowboy appeared and refused to pay the $2 cover. He was wearing a big white hat and the girl working at the door came and told me that this white guy refused to pay the cover and insisted on being let in free, so I told Abel to go over and check things out. By this time, the Anglo cowboy had walked into the place and Abel met him at the door, put up his hands, and said, 'wait a minute, nobody comes in without paying the cover.' 'Meskin, I don't pay to enter any Meskin place,' the white guy said. Man, Abel reached inside his coat and pulled out his 45 and hit that white boy three times in the head and knocked him out. I heard the commotion and ran over and said, 'Abel, what the hell happened?' and he said, 'Nobody calls me a Meskin and gets away with it,' and then he told me what happened. Man, that cowboy was crazy for calling Abel a Meskin because Abel was a little crazy himself." Everyone chuckles at the story.

A colleague suggested the utterance of "Meskin" among the Mexican patrons might not always be intentional. She brought to my attention the difficulty that some Mexicans have pronouncing the 'x' in English and the tendency to give it an 's' sound, especially if they grew up speaking Spanish, and she gave herself as an example.

"In the past, every time when I said Mexican it sounded like Meskin and one time my daughter told me not to use it because it was derogatory. I was shocked because I had been saying Meskin all these years. Now when I say Mexican, I slow down and say it correctly."

This accent implication was noticeable in a few of the patrons, but it is also true that the term was likewise deliberately used, and that both the Mexican and white patrons were aware of its negative connotations. What follows are examples of how the patrons continually used the term Meskin as a social construction through their interactions.

Meskins and Social Class

The first time I heard the term in the bar was early in my visits in a discussion with the octogenarian Mr. Charlie about his long history of residence in Second Ward. He showed a group of us the social security card that he had received in 1936. His name included both his mother's and father's surnames. We marveled at the fact that he still had his original social security card, and someone mentioned that the use of both parents' last names was a Mexican tradition. Mr. Charlie acknowledged as much and JB immediately chimed in. "I thought you told me you were white," he said, "but you're nothing but a damn Meskin just like the rest of us." We laughed. I relayed to everyone that Mr. Charlie was a historical figure because he was one of the few original residents of Second Ward still living. "A historical giant," Harvey said laughing. "Yeah, and a Meskin to boot," JB followed, "none of this white shit." We laughed again. In telling Mr. Charlie that he was "nothing but a damn Meskin just like the rest of us," JB compared Mr. Charlie's fate to that of all Meskins, and although he did not define what kind of fate he had in mind, he implied a lower working-class status with all of the attendant social issues. This was why Meskins were "damned."

On another occasion JB used the term as a descriptor of a working-class lifestyle and values. One afternoon he was talking about his weekend visit to the rodeo on Go Tejano Day, when the Houston Livestock Show and Rodeo focused on Tejano culture and music. JB's comments made it clear he was identifying with the Mexican working-class culture. It was also obvious he found pleasure in doing so.

> "Yeah, so we were walking and looking around, you know, taking it all in, the booths and everything, and when we walked by this one place and heard this Meskin music with an accordion and everything I said 'oh, oh.' So, we walked in and sat down and ordered a beer, and then another and another, and before you know it, I'm dancing with my old lady and her sister and having a good time. Man, I didn't think I would wind up drinking and dancing on a Sunday evening, but you know how us Meskins can be."

Meskin music in JB's terms referenced the traditional conjunto style of music that originated among the working class in Texas (Pena 1985). According to JB it was irresistible because Meskins liked to dance and drink, even on a Sunday afternoon. That Meskins favor pleasure, as JB implied, is a stereotype of long standing (De Leon 1983).

A class distinction was made more explicit in another exchange between Geraldo and White Mike. Geraldo juxtaposed Meskin with Hispanic and challenged Mike's use of the term Hispanic. A group of patrons was on the deck, and Mike was talking about his neighborhood and the school district in Pasadena, a small city near Houston that had been transformed by "the Hispanic population." Mike's use of the term "Hispanic" was followed quickly by a question from Geraldo.

> "Do you mean Meskin or Hi-spanic?" Geraldo asks, emphasizing the first two letters in the term Hispanic. Mike ignores the question and continues to talk about his neighborhood and how it had changed from being white to predominately Hispanic. "Are you talking about Meskins or Hi-spanics?" Geraldo asks again in a loud voice. Mike stares at Geraldo for a moment and then responds, "Okay, Meskins, but I tell you they have really changed the place."

By emphasizing the "Hi" in Hispanic and contrasting it with the term Meskin, Geraldo invoked the image of two classes—the professional, middle-class Hispanic and the working and poorer Meskin classes—and he pushed Mike to make the distinction. "Okay, Meskins," Mike declared after Geraldo's insistence, acquiescing to the more accurate descriptor implied by Geraldo's question. Did Mike use the term Hispanic to be polite? His terminology was uncharacteristic for he usually used the term Meskin (see below). The population of Pasadena had grown largely due to the influx of immigrants from Mexico and a growing population of U.S.-born Mexicans, and perhaps Geraldo felt Mike was being patronizing by using the term Hispanic. Mike initially ignored Geraldo's distinction, indicating that perhaps he did not want to be exposed as condescending. Regardless, Mike understood the distinction when he said in a tone of surrender, "Okay, Meskins."

Meskins as a Tribe

When the Mexican patrons referred to themselves as Meskin, they used it as an affectionate in-group term that expressed solidarity and bonding. JB's comments cited earlier were indicative. A more explicit incident of in-group affection occurred one afternoon. Several Mexican patrons were sitting on the deck discussing their marriages, and the conversation segued into comments about marriage expectations while growing up. Putting down his beer, Johnny started the conversation.

"Marrying a Meskin used to be a big deal when I was growing up but it's no longer a big deal anymore. You see Meskins married to all kinds of people now," he says. "When I was growing up my mother always told me to marry a Meskin," Jessie Jr. chimes in. "'Don't marry anyone else,' she would tell me, and sometimes she would say that she would disown me if I married anybody but a Meskin, so you know, I never thought about marrying anyone else." "Yeah, I know what you mean," Robert says. "I grew up wanting to marry a Meskin and I did and I'm glad I did. I always wanted to marry a Meskin." "That was the same with me," Johnny says. "I grew up wanting to marry a Meskin because you just knew that was what you were supposed to do and that is what I did, hell, twice." He laughs. "You knew you were not supposed to marry a colored or a white person, it had to be a Meskin, but now even that's changed, and I think it's better because, you know, you should be able to marry who you want." "Yeah, but I still prefer a Meskin," Jessie Jr. says. "Me too," Robert chimes in.

Preference for a Meskin bride was expressed as a strong in-group norm and as such was an example of endogamy. Every racial group in society is an in-group unto themselves and others are the out-group. In-groups always prefer their own, and thus it was with the Meskin patrons on the deck. One was expected to marry a Meskin. They were socialized into this expectation and warned about consequences if they didn't, but it was what they wanted and what they did and it made them feel good, and if it didn't work out the first time, well, try again with another member of the ethnic group, another Meskin. The strength of the norm was clearly expressed when it was said, "My mother always told me to marry a Meskin," "I never thought of marrying anyone else," and "I grew up wanting to marry a Meskin and I'm glad I did." Johnny, however, recognized that the norm was changing. In-group commitment lessens with each succeeding genera-tion, especially in mixed-racial cities like Houston where opportunity for interactions with others is common. Some Meskins, however, continued to prefer their own, regardless of their Americanization and changed norms, as indicated by Jessie Jr. and Robert. Johnny, however, saw change and was open. "I think it's better," he said, "you should be able to marry who you want." Yet the prevailing sentiment in the bar tended to be endogamous and expressed through their use of Meskin as a self-referent, as seen in the following exchanges.

One evening while sitting at the bar, Kid was asked by a young white woman to play "some Spanish music" on the jukebox. "There ain't any Spaniards or Spanish music in this place," Kid said in a somewhat stern, matter-of-fact manner. "There ain't nothing but Meskins and Meskin music in here. This is a Meskin place." "Oh, sorry," she replied and slowly ambled away. Another interaction involving Kid occurred early one afternoon.

Kid walks in and greets everyone at the domino table. He makes his way
down the bar shaking hands. When he gets to Mr. Jim he says, "Do you
need anything?" "No," Mr. Jim says, "I'm fine." "Good," Kid says, "because
I don't want you to need anything because Meskins treat white people
right in here and we don't want you out there on the street saying that we
Meskins don't know how to treat white people." Mr. Jim smiles.

In another instance White Mike and Wiley were discussing the beginning of deer season and the discussion turned to butchering deer. A small
group of Mexican patrons were listening.

"I never cut all the meat off a deer," Mike says, "it's not worth the effort. I
only take what's around the spine." "I take everything," Wiley says. "I don't
leave anything." "You think like a Meskin and Mike thinks like a white
man because Meskins eat everything," Gilbert tells Wiley. "Well then, I
must be a Meskin because I leave very little meat on a deer once I kill it,"
Wiley responds.

Kid's remarks to the young white woman and Mr. Jim were in-group
cultural markers: "Meskin music" in a Meskin place and "Meskin" respect
for white people. Gilbert's comments to Wiley had social-class connotations. "Meskins" were of the lower working class and hence would not leave
any meat on a deer as it represented food for another meal.

Meskins as a Matter of Fact

The white patrons also used the term "Meskin" in a normal and ordinary
fashion, as part of their everyday language and in a matter-of-fact manner.
It made clear the other group implications. Once when Mr. Jim walked
in, Phil, one of the Mexican patrons, told Efren, "Your brother is here." Mr.
Jim laughed and replied, "I don't have any Meskin brothers." White Mike
used the term more frequently than the other white patrons and used it to
describe food, bars, patrons, families, and the community at large. The following are a few examples of White Mike's use of the term.

I ask Mike about his weekend and he says that he and his wife ate "Meskin food" at the Last Concert, a popular café on the north side of Houston. Mike is describing a biker bar located somewhere in the East End. "It ain't a Meskin bar or anything like that," he says.

Mike and several of his pipe-fitter coworkers are sitting on the deck. I approach and shake hands with each of them and exchange greetings. "Who is inside?" I ask him. "Just a bunch of Meskins," he responds.

Mike is talking about getting his hair cut over the weekend and says, "yeah, this ole Meskin guy cuts my hair."

Some patrons are talking about their Christmas Day plans. Mike says that he will be at his mother-in-law's home and that they will eat, open gifts, and leave as soon as they can. "Hell, we're not like Meskin families," he says, "you like to visit and hang around your families. White people are not like that. We hate our families and the less time we must spend around them, the better. Meskins like their families."

Mike is talking with Gabriel about a coworker and describes him as having a heavy Meskin accent. "I'm glad you have a neutral accent," another patron tells him. We laugh. "I know I have a heavy southern accent," Mike says. "Meskins are not the only ones with accents."

Mike's son, Matthew, joins the domino game for the first time ever and immediately starts winning. "Damn," someone says, "he picked up the game quick." "We play it all the time at school," Matthews says. "He goes to Pasadena High and there's nothing but Meskins there," Mike says. "Yeah," Matthew responds, "there are a few whites there, maybe two." We laugh. "He's been around Meskins all his life," Mike says. "I sure have," Matthew says, "I'm not *estupido*." We laugh again.

Mike tells a story about a "Meskin" who stole his truck and how he was teased by a coworker who told him, "Now Mikey boy, let me get this straight, you let a Meskin steal your truck?"

Mike says that he sees where his tax dollars are going every day when he sees the Meskins walking to school in Pasadena.

Given White Mike's frequent use of the term, I sought to ascertain his awareness of its negative connotation. One afternoon a group of patrons were on the deck talking about Mr. Charlie's reputation as a hustler when the topic turned to the various labels used to identify Mexicans. White Mike and Paul were the only two white patrons present.

> "Yeah," Fi says laughing, "that damn Mexican has always been that way." "Now the ole man doesn't claim to be Mexican, he claims to be white," JB chimes in. "White my ass," Fi says laughing, "ese viejito es mas Mexicano que la chingada" (that old man is more Mexican than anything). "Hell, I've been everything," JB continues. "I used to be white when I was in the Marine Corps. They had me fill out a form and I marked 'other' and the sergeant who gave me the form said, 'no you're white,' so I put white. I think I even have a driver's license that says I'm white, and when I got out of the Marines, they were calling us Chicanos." "I know, I know," Fi says, "it's the same thing with me—first I was white, then I was Mexican American, and then Chicano." "And now you're Hispanic," White Mike interjects, "and the white man's burden." We laugh. "Yeah, Hispanic came later, in fact just recently," Fi says. "It sounds to me like you Meskins have an identity problem," Mike continues laughing. "How do you spell that?" I ask. "What?" he asks. "Meskin," I reply, "how do you spell it?" "M-E-S-K-I-N," he responds quickly in a loud voice. He and Paul laugh and give each other a high five. "You know what Shakespeare said?" I reply. "What's that?" Mike asks. "A Mexican by any other name is still a Mexican," I respond. "Shakespeare my ass," he says laughing.

Mike quickly realized that I was referencing the term's negative connotation, but he did not back down. He knew the term was derogatory and spelled it out forcefully to make the point. Paul showed similar knowledge by joining Mike in the spontaneous, celebratory, and victorious high five, a display of triumphant body language. We know the term is negative, they were messaging, and don't care if you and the others know it.

Jerry and Mr. Jim, two of the white patrons, also used "Meskin," but perhaps not as frequently as White Mike. The following story was told by Jerry about Mr. Jim. In his narrative, they both used the term Meskin but with different meanings. A group of patrons were on the deck when someone mentioned that Mr. Jim had not been to the bar recently. Jerry was the only white patron present.

> "Hell, just last week I saved his ass," Jerry says. "We were drinking at the D&W and the Meskins were there drinking and ole Jim had them blocked in with that old car of his, and some Meskins wanted to leave but they couldn't find out who had them blocked in, so I went outside and saw that old black car he drives and went back inside and told him that he needed to move his car because some Meskins wanted to leave, and he started cussing, saying, 'Fuck those goddamn Meskins, I don't have to move for those motherfuckers,' and I told him that he better move or they will move it for you, and he looked at me and I said 'I'm serious, you better move your car or those Meskins will move it for you. You don't want to fuck with them.' 'Well those goddamn Meskins better not mess with me,' he said, but he finally got up and moved his car."

In telling this story, Jerry used Meskin in a casual manner, as a normal, matter-of-fact moniker. He quoted Mr. Jim as using the term in a negative and angry tone by prefacing it with profanity. He called Meskins sexual deviants and invoked God to damn them and said that they "better not mess with me." Of course, Mr. Jim relented and moved his car because he didn't want the "goddamn Meskins" to mess with him.

Only once during my visits did I hear the term "Meskin" questioned, and it again involved Mr. Jim. The bar was crowded when he walked in with his cane and started complaining.

> "Some damn Meskin took my parking space," he says out loud as he slowly makes his way to a stool. JB looks up from behind the bar and says in a serious tone, "You must be talking about some other place, white man, because there ain't any damn Meskins in here." Mr. Jim does not respond.

These exchanges illustrated the sociological truism that context determines meaning. In both examples, Mr. Jim cursed the Meskins, but in the first instance not in front of them. In the second example, however, he cursed them in front of JB. He damned the Meskins in a negative tone and received repudiation from JB, who used context in reminding Mr. Jim of his whiteness and his physical whereabouts.

The Rituals of Mr. Charlie

Mr. Charlie was the son of one of the first Mexican families to move into Second Ward in the 1920s when the barrio was just beginning to form. His real name was Jose, but he said he started calling himself Charlie because "back then I didn't have much of a chance as Jose." The only time during his eighty-nine years that Mr. Charlie did not live in Second Ward was when he was in the military for three years during World War II. He knew everyone in the bar, and many of them since birth, and he knew their fathers and mothers. He had been around Mexicans all his life not only as a resident of Second Ward but also as a member of a Mexican golf association and as coach of a Mexican baseball team. He spoke Spanish and was married to a Mexican woman. Yet, despite his Mexican heritage, Mr. Charlie constantly asserted that he was a white American and ridiculed everything Mexican by referring to them as Meskins and peppers and insisting that neither of these labels applied to him because he was a member of the white race. Mr. Charlie deliberately used Meskin to generate laughter. Often, he walked into the bar and asked JB if he had any "Meskin soda water," referring to the Mexican mineral water that JB sold. When patrons made comments to him in Spanish, he would reply that he didn't "speak or understand much Meskin," which, of course, was not true. On one occasion Mr. Charlie walked in, shook hands with everyone, and greeted them in Spanish with "como estas" (how are you) and "con mucho gusto" (it's a pleasure), and then laughed and said in English, "Damn, I can talk that Meskin pretty good." When JB and Efren referred to each other as "mi compadre lindo" (my cute friend), Mr. Charlie would laugh and say they talked to each other as boyfriend and girlfriend and "they do it in Meskin." Sometimes he used the term to refer to Mike's utterance of the few Spanish words he had learned in the bar. At the end of a domino game, Mr. Charlie would utter *ya estufas*, a slang term from the Pachuco era meaning "it's over" or "it's done" (Galvan and Teschner 1995). When he drew dominoes out of turn, JB pulled them back, saying, "etiquette, old man, etiquette." "Etiquette mis huevos" (my balls) Mr. Charlie would reply and draw his dominoes anyway. White Mike learned these terms and often he and Mr. Charlie would say "ya estufas" and "etiquette mis huevos" simultaneously and then laugh. White Mike also referred to JB as "Chuy," the nickname in Spanish for Jesse, and he called black people "mayates," a negative slang term in Spanish. When these rituals occurred, Mr. Charlie laughed and often said, "Listen to ole White Mike speak Meskin" or "Listen to ole Meskin Mike," to which White Mike usually responded with "Hell, you can't help but learn some Meskin if you come here long enough." Mr. Charlie also called Mexicans "peppers," one of the staples of the Mexican diet. To Mr. Charlie the pepper stood as the defining Mexican symbol, and he used it as a ridiculing analogy so often that when other patrons questioned him about his Mexican heritage, they likewise used the term, as in "Why do you deny that you are a pepper?" On one occasion when Mr. Charlie entered the bar, JB greeted him as follows:

> "How you doing Jose, or is Joe? Hell, you have so many names I don't know what to call you, but it doesn't make any difference because regardless you're still a pepper." "Did you hear that?" Mr. Charlie asks the patrons. "Now tell me, who looks like a pepper, me or Jesse Jr.?" He laughs. "I don't care what you call me," he says, "because I know I'm cute." We laugh. "Makes love more binding," Mr. Charlie responds.

Mr. Charlie's constant assertion of being white included "I'm free and white" or "I'm four times 21 and white." He usually uttered these phrases when he was told that he could not do something. Once he joined a group on the deck and sat in JB's favorite chair. When JB came out of the bar and onto the deck he asked Mr. Charlie, "Who gave you permission to sit in my chair?" "I don't need permission," Mr. Charlie responded. "I'm free and white and four times 21 and can do what the hell I want." JB bantered back but he did not make Mr. Charlie move.

A composite description follows that captures Mr. Charlie's assertions

of being white and his use of the terms "Meskin" and "pepper" to refer to
Mexicans. These mini-dramas were rituals that often occurred before large
audiences who were entertained by his antics. Mr. Charlie was socially constructing himself as white and rejecting his Mexican heritage.

> The bar is full when Mr. Charlie walks in. He goes through the bar shaking
> hands and exchanging greetings and then heads towards the domino
> table. "Is ole what's-his-name going to play?" he asks in a loud enough
> voice for JB to hear. "Yeah," JB says, "but only if you don't start telling me
> that you're white. I don't want to hear all that white shit." Mr. Charlie
> ignores the remark and invites me to play. "I hope I don't lose my lunch
> money," I say as I sit down. "Don't you worry," Mr. Charlie responds, "I'll
> take care of you. Do you want an American or Meskin sandwich?" "What's
> a Meskin sandwich?" I ask. "A taco," he responds laughing, "but I don't eat
> them. I eat American sandwiches. I'm not like that guy over there that
> eats all that pepper stuff." He motions to Efren, who is making his way to
> the table. "Listen ole man," Efren says in an aggressive tone, "I'm a damn
> proud Mexican, I'm not like you." "I know," Mr. Charlie responds, wink-
> ing at me, "but this is America not Mexico and I'm an American, a white
> American." "Yeah, yeah," Efren responds, "you're nothing but a fucking
> wetback." We laugh. "You're the only wetback in here," Mr. Charlie retorts,
> "and an ordinary one at that." Efren does not respond. We take our seats
> and start the game. I win several hands in a row, and each time JB tells me
> that he is letting me win by playing the numbers that I have in my hand.
> "Why don't you let me win?" Mr. Charlie asks JB, "I thought we were cous-
> ins?" "Now, how in the hell can we be cousins," JB replies, "with you being
> white and all, because I'm sure as hell not white." "Well, then we may not
> be related then because I *am* white," Mr. Charlie responds. "Yeah," JB says,
> "white like my brown ass." We laugh. "Ain't this awful," Mr. Charlie replies.
> JB goes on a winning streak while Mr. Charlie loses several games in a
> row. Efren begins to taunt him because he knows that Mr. Charlie hates to
> lose. "Chingale compadre" (screw him, my friend) Efren tells JB over and
> over, "chingale el viejito" (screw the old man), "chingale compadre." "Do
> you know what he is saying?" Mr. Charlie asks me, "I don't because I don't

speak pepper." "The hell you don't," Efren says, "you're the biggest wetback pepper in here." Mr. Charlie ignores the remark. Mr. Jim comes hobbling into the bar and makes his way to an empty stool and sits down. "JB," Mr. Charlie says out loud, "go take care of Jim, give him whatever he wants. Jim, just let me know if you need anything." "And what the hell will you do if I don't?" JB asks. "Just take care of Jim," Mr. Charlie responds. "Hell, Jim and I are the only white people in here." "Yeah, like I said, you ole buzzard, you're white just like my brown ass." We laugh. "I don't care what you say about me because I know I'm cute," Mr. Charlie replies. Kid walks to the domino table, stands beside Mr. Charlie, and begins to talk to JB about an incident at his job. Mr. Charlie loses the game, reaches into his pocket, and takes out his money clip. Kid acts as if to grab the clip and brushes Mr. Charlie's shoulder. "Uh, uh," Mr. Charlie says quickly, moving his money clip away. "You have no damn business touching a white man and trying to take his money." Kid laughs. "White man my ass," he says, "you're nothing but a stone Meskin, always have been and always will be." "Not me," Mr. Charlie responds, "I'm white. Now you may be a pepper but not me. I'm a white American, always have been and always will be." "Yeah, yeah," Kid responds. Mr. Charlie starts winning and his mood brightens. "What happened to *chingale, chingale* and all that pepper talk," he asks Efren, while laughing after winning a game. "Fuck you, ole man," Efren says. "Chingale, chingale," Mr. Charlie says again, laughing. "Fucking wetback," Efren mutters. "You're the only wetback in here and, like I said, an ordinary pepper at that," Mr. Charlie responds. Efren does not reply. We play in silence for a few moments. A cumbia starts playing on the jukebox and Mr. Charlie begins swaying back and forth. "I thought you didn't like pepper music?" Kid tells him. "I don't," Mr. Charlie says, "I like American music." He pauses for a moment and then asks, "Is that pepper music? If it is, I may have to start listening because it sounds pretty good." He laughs. At the end of one game, Efren accuses Mr. Charlie of not paying him. The game stops as they argue. "Let's play the game," JB says. Mr. Charlie slides a quarter hard across the table towards Efren. "I'm not going hang around here and give my money away to some damn pepper," he says. "I'll leave." "Fuck you, you damn wetback," Efren responds in an angry tone. The game resumes.

Efren plays a few more games and then quits. White Mike takes his place and immediately wins several games in a row. "Damn, it must be affirmative action," Kid says. "You're damn right," White Mike says, "I'm the only white person in this place." "No, you're not," Mr. Charlie responds, "I'm white." "Yeah," White Mike responds, "you're white like JB is white." We laugh. We play in silence for a few seconds and then Mr. Charlie asks, "Isn't this the day that they holler and all that?" "Who?" I ask. "The peppers," he responds, "isn't this the day they have a parade and yell and scream?" "Oh, you mean Mexican Independence Day," I answer. "Yeah," he says, "that's all you see on television is that it's pepper day." "Oh, Mr. Charlie," Denise says from the bar, "why do you call them peppers? Aren't you a pepper?" "He's the biggest pepper in Second Ward," JB says, "always has been and always will be." "You hear that nonsense, Tatcho?" Mr. Charlie says, "ole Jessie Jr. here calling me a pepper. Now tell me, who looks like a pepper, me or Jessie Jr. here?" "Don't you speak pepper?" Denise asks. "Yeah, I speak a little bit," Mr. Charlie responds, "but I picked it up in this old dump; hell you can't come in here without picking up some pepper because this is a pepper place, but I'm white." "Jose the only thing white about you is your damn lies," JB tells him. We laugh. "Yeah, they used to call me Jose," Mr. Charlie responds, "but I changed it because I'm an American, a white American. Now you may be Hispanic and all that *quacha* [bullshit], but not me, I'm white." "Yeah, yeah," JB says. Mr. Charlie goes on a winning streak and wins four games in a row. After his fourth win, he says "Asi baila mija con el senor" (that's how the little girl dances with the gentleman). "I thought you didn't speak pepper," Leo tells him from the bar. "I don't," Mr. Charlie says, "it just came out." "Did you hear that?" Leo asks everyone loudly. "Mr. Charlie's pepper came out. Don't be taking your pepper out in here." Everyone laughs.

Mr. Charlie knew his assertion about being white drew laughter, and no doubt, that was his intent. Initially I believed his assertions about whiteness were simply another of his many rituals to make people laugh, but over time I reconsidered. Mr. Charlie, like many other Mexican patrons in the bar, was extremely patriotic. He was proud to have been born in the United

States as an American citizen and to have served in the Navy during World War II. He repeatedly mentioned his experiences in the Navy and talked about his two favorite presidents, Franklin Delano Roosevelt and Harry Truman. He liked President Roosevelt because "he gave us Social Security; before then it was root hog or die." President Truman was a favorite because "he dropped the bomb and ended the war. He did what he had to do." During serious conversations when I asked about his ethnic identity, he always replied, "I'm an American, a white American, always have been and always will be," and he never once wavered and was sincere in his assertion. Mr. Charlie may not have believed he was white in the same sense the white patrons were white, but he felt he was part of the white race, perhaps because he conflated American citizenship and whiteness. They meant the same thing and overlapped in his self-conception. This conflation was discovered to be more common than anticipated. Research illustrates that American-born Mexicans, especially later generations, tended to fuse citizenship and notions of whiteness into their identity. Once their Mexican identity faded, it was replaced by a white identity (Vasquez 2010; Murguia and Telles 1996). Mr. Charlie was a second-generation Mexican, and his assertion of whiteness was perhaps the harbinger of how future generations would assert their racial affiliation.

In contrast to Mr. Charlie's assertions of whiteness, there was the patron Duck, and his efforts to break through his whiteness to prove he was a Mexican. Duck was very light-skinned and had light-colored hair and eyes. When I first saw him in the bar, I thought he was white, but I later learned that he was a Mexican. One evening during a conversation I learned that he had experienced problems because of his white skin. He began by telling me about the Doghouse, a tavern where he used to work as a bartender. He described it as a place of action. I asked how he found the Doghouse and the story he told involved his white complexion.

"I went there with a friend of mine and I remember this little gangster came up and said, 'what the hell are you doing here white boy,' and I said, 'fuck you, I'm no white boy, I'm a Mexican, a Chicano,' and he said, 'well you sure as hell look like a white boy to me, so why are you trying to pass yourself off as a Mexican?' We kept going back and forth and, man, we were getting ready to get into it when Alfredo, the owner, walked over and told the punk to cool it, and the punk started to tell Alfredo something but Alfredo grabbed him and took him to the door and threw him out. Man, I've been getting that white boy shit all my life, so it was nothing new, but damn, you know, you get tired of it, people thinking that you are white all the time. I used to get it at school all the time from both the *gabachos* [whites] asking why I said I was Mexican and Mexicans thinking that I was white, and I'd get in more shit because people wouldn't believe that I was Mexican."

Duck was a man in between, a Mexican with a white complexion. He grew up in a Mexican neighborhood, had Mexican friends, married a brown-skinned Mexican woman, but he looked white. He could have easily passed, but he did not want to escape his Mexicanness and instead sought to embrace and live it, but this effort had long caused him grief because neither Mexicans nor whites believed he was a Mexican.

Discussion

Regionalism and the relative lack of sting from the slur "Meskin" made it easier for the patrons to use the term, but with differences. The Mexicans appropriated it and undermined its negativity by using it as an in-group term of pride and solidarity. Similar appropriation of other words such as the N-word by African Americans (Asim 2007) and queer by the LGBT community have given them a positive in-group meaning. The appropriation of Meskin by the Mexican patrons contributed to making it easier for the whites to use the term. Context, however, is important in determining the term's offensiveness. This was shown in JB's stern retort to Mr. Jim's complaint that some "damn Meskin" took his parking place. Compare this with the context in which JB referred to Mr. Charlie as a "damn Meskin" in the discussion dealing with Mr. Charlie's social security card. This context was humorous, and the speaker was JB, another Mexican, whereas in the example between JB and Mr. Jim, the context was serious, and the profanity came from a white patron. Yet, despite contextual issues, the term "Meskin" alone does not carry the same negativity of "greaser" and "spic," and this likewise made it easier to use the term.

Whiteness has always been an issue within the Mexican population because their complexion hues range from dark brown to white, as in the case of Duck (Chacon Mendoza 2008; Cuéllar, Maldonado, and Roberts 1997; Michelson 2003). White-skinned Mexicans have a history of being acceptable to other whites. When Mexicans were called mongrels by white immigrants in the 1820s, the light-skinned were being courted by the same immigrants as business partners, political allies, and spouses (De Leon 1983).

Mexicans also have a history of going to court to have themselves declared part of the white race (De Leon 2000; Garcia 2009; Cantrell 2013), and many mark "white" on the census form when answering the race question. A special Census tabulation in 2000 illustrated that 63 percent of Texas Mexicans marked "white" in comparison to 45 percent who lived in the other southwestern states (Tafoya 2004). Some have argued that Mexicans who live along the Texas border are prone to emphasize being part of the white race more than in other southwestern states because of their desire to draw a distinction between themselves and Mexicans from Mexico (Overmyer-Velazquez 2013). When Mexicans were asked to describe their skin color, 41 percent said light, 28 percent medium brown, and 30 percent dark-skinned. When others described their skin color, the figures were 26 percent light-skinned, 45 percent medium brown, and 29 percent dark-skinned (Murguia and Telles 1996). The truth is probably somewhere in between these descriptions, but the point is that the Mexicans who marked white on the U.S. Census form and described their skin color as white may truly believe they are part of the Caucasian race but not identify as Anglo-Saxons, as may be the case with Mr. Charlie. Whiteness is an issue not only among Mexicans in the United States, but also in Mexico, where the light-skinned are favored and comprise the elite class. Indeed, it is an issue in all countries where people of different hues live, usually with the white-skinned governing the darker-skinned.

CHAPTER FIVE

African Americans

D o the norms that restrain negative comments about other racial groups represent a decline in prejudiced behavior? Critics are not sure because there is a difference between what people say and how they feel and behave. Indirect measures of prejudice such as social distance scales indicate that prejudice among whites in the United States has declined within the last sixty years. More whites than ever before say they would not oppose living in the same neighborhood with minorities (Weaver 2008) and Houston appears to have followed the trend. The annual Kinder Houston Area Survey has frequently asked whites if they preferred to live in an all-white, mostly white, mixed half-and-half, mostly black, or all-black neighborhood. In 1985 only 27 percent of whites said they preferred to live in an integrated, half-white and half-black neighborhood. In 2001, the percentage increased to an impressive 60 percent. Those who said they preferred to live in an all-white neighborhood declined from 31 percent to less than 8 percent. Yet the research also reports that during the same period, residential segregation between whites and African Americans in Houston increased (Klineberg 2005). This might be a consequence of

Houston being a low-density city, the report speculated, because Houston covers a large geographical area. Thus, there is a greater probability that residential enclaves based on social class and race would develop due to more space. Perhaps, but Houston may also be following a national trend. A 2012 National Associated Press poll reported the number of people that expressed negative feelings toward African Americans increased from 48 percent in 2008 to 51 percent in 2012. Implicit or unconscious feelings of prejudice increased during the same period from 49 percent to 56 percent. President Obama's election may have increased prejudice rather than fostering an era of racial conciliation as some have suggested (Goldman 2012). More whites were being vocal about their prejudice because they resented the election of an African American as their president.

Research dealing with white prejudice is extensive, but it is only recently that the prejudices of Mexicans and African Americans have begun to receive attention. Indeed, as Perlmutter (2002) pointed out, it has been a "no-no" to suggest minorities could be prejudiced towards whites and other minorities. Perlmutter, however, did not draw a distinction between prejudice and discrimination. Prejudice refers to negative feelings towards another group, while discrimination refers to behavior that treats other groups unfairly because of their race, gender, religion, etc. Mexicans and other minorities can indeed be prejudiced, but their ability to discriminate is limited because they do not hold positions of authority on a scale that gives them the power to act against others. Thus, it would be more accurate to say minorities can indeed hold prejudiced views toward other groups, but to assert they have the power to discriminate would be a no-no because of their limited ability to do so.

Most Hispanics (the majority being Mexican) and African Americans in Houston have defined their relationship with each other as good (Mindiola, Niemann, and Rodriguez 2002). Both groups were not opposed to working with the other, living in the same neighborhoods, or sending their children to the same schools. Nor were they opposed to their children having friends from the other group; however, if the relationship involved dating and marriage, a majority in each group were opposed, with more Hispanics than African Americans opposed.

A minority in each group also perceived each other in negative terms, but more Hispanics were negative in their perceptions. This was especially true of immigrants. The issues of contention between the two groups were immigration and language. African Americans believed that immigrants took their jobs, and they opposed the speaking of Spanish in the workplace. When asked if they believed their community was prejudiced against African Americans, a quarter of the native-born and over 40 percent of foreign-born Hispanics responded affirmatively.

Research has also reported that both dark- and light-skinned Hispanics practiced "colorism," meaning within their own group they were more favorably disposed toward the light- over the dark-skinned members (Uhlmann et al. 2002). Given this, prejudiced feelings about African Americans among Mexicans should not be surprising. Some scholars have argued that conflict between the two groups was becoming more prevalent because the size of the Mexican population had increased to the point where they were now the largest minority group in the United States, a status long held by African Americans. The presumed alliance between Mexicans and African Americans that had rested upon a shared minority status, therefore, was fraying as Mexicans increasingly competed with African Americans for housing, education, jobs, and political influence (Vaca 2004). The states of California, South Carolina, New Jersey, and Washington, for example, have reported conflict between Mexicans and African Americans (Buchanan 2005). The conflict in Houston has been minimal, and as stated, both groups held positive views of each other (Rodriguez and Mindiola 2011). These positive views, however, rarely surfaced among JB's Mexican patrons, who were in concert with the white patrons in their negative views about African Americans.

African American Patrons

The only African American who patronized the bar on a regular basis was Big Al, a 6 foot, 9 inches tall, 350-pound police officer who had been a patron for eight years. Big Al came to the bar as a result of his affiliation with the

Silver Bullet Pigs, a cooking team that included several police officers who were JB's patrons. The team engaged in benefit cooking for police officers who were facing financial emergencies. JB was one of their sponsors and he helped with the cooking when their fundraising events were held at his place. Big Al said the cooking team always talked about JB's Drive Inn and he eventually accompanied them to the bar, had a good time, and has been a patron ever since. Big Al was affable. He joked with everyone, played dominoes, put money in the jukebox, shared his buckets of beer, and took orders for his mother's homemade pies, which he delivered to the bar. At times, there were several weeks between Big Al's visits, but there were also times when he came on a more regular basis. His police colleagues said Big Al "only hangs out with Mexicans."

Five other African Americans—Wulf, Jackie, Double Yolk Man, Chuck, and Chris—made occasional forays into the bar. Wulf worked with Kid, JB's brother, and Jackie worked with JB's son, JB Jr. They visited the bar on several occasions after their work hours and sat outside on the deck drinking and talking. Double Yolk Man came by the bar every few weeks on Friday evenings selling brown eggs with double yolks in quantities of no less than two dozen. JB always loudly announced his presence with "Double Yolk Man is here!" Sometimes Double Yolk Man made sales and sometimes not, but apparently the sales he did make were enough to keep him showing up every few weeks and becoming known to the patrons.

Chuck owned a manufacturing firm across the street, and though his visits were infrequent, usually to purchase bottled water, a few times he sat on the deck and drank a beer with the patrons. Consequently, he was involved in two incidents of race talk. During a domino game, Mike mentioned that Chuck would not call him White Mike. When he was asked why, Mike responded as follows.

> "I don't know, I guess because he's black and feels uncomfortable, but he told me he could not call me White Mike, but I can call him Black Chuck," he says laughing and slamming down a domino.

There was a time in America when African Americans had to be extremely deferential to whites at the risk of their lives. They had to be very careful when speaking to or even looking at a white person, and these proscriptions were especially strict when it came to African American men and white women. This history, I venture to say, was informing and reflecting Chuck's sentiments. He may have felt that using White Mike's nickname crossed a prohibited racial boundary that an African American male should not cross because it would be making fun of a white man and this was dangerous.

Chuck's other racial exchange occurred with Leo, one of the Mexican patrons. One afternoon Leo told a small group that he and Chuck had been conversing on the deck the previous evening. He had asked Chuck if he could use extra workers at his plant because several men from his local union were looking for part-time work. Chuck said he could because the African American males he had working for him were lazy. Leo said that he started to agree by using the N-word but then caught himself and said nothing. Chuck realized Leo's hesitation and told him to go ahead and use the term. Leo said he hesitated for a moment but then complied with "okay, niggahs are lazy." Leo laughed as he told the story and then described Chuck as a "pretty good black guy," presumably because he gave him permission to use the N-word.

Chris was part of a mixed racial group that visited on Friday nights. His girlfriend was a Mexican, and their group included two unattached Mexican males and another Mexican female whose husband was white. Chris joined the domino game on two occasions, but for the most part he remained with his group. He was, however, involved in a race-talk incident with Leo. One evening Leo asked me if I knew Chris. I said yes, and he relayed the following story and laughed heartily when he finished. He did not say how Chris or the other members of the group reacted.

> "Well, when I was bartending for JB last Friday night, Chris came in with his group and I pulled out the gun that JB has under the bar and told him, "Damn, Chris, I saw a nigger walk in and I thought I was going to get robbed so I pulled out this gun before I realized it was you."

Leo was mocking real-life circumstances. When people see an African American male, their first reaction is negative with assessment coming afterwards (Oliver 2003).

The N-Word

Although African Americans were for the most part physically absent from the bar, they were nevertheless *there* in the minds and lexicon of the Mexican and white patrons. They repeatedly engaged in microaggressions that made African Americans the butt of jokes and described them in negative, stereotypical terms, such as thieves, dumb, lazy, untrustworthy, complainers, and prone to use the race card. Indicative of their prejudiced feelings was their consistent use of the slur "nigger," the most controversial and provocative racial slur in American history. As scholars have noted, it is "the nuclear bomb of racial epithets" (Kennedy 2002; Asim 2007). A few times the patrons used "nigga," as illustrated above by Leo, but "nigger" was the more common description.

The N-word is reported to have its roots in either Latin (Asim 2007) or the Spanish language (Kennedy 2002). In each language, the term referred to the color black—*niger* in Latin and *negro* in Spanish. Over time, the term morphed into "nigger," but no one seems to know how or why. Linguist Jacquelyn Rahman (2012), in her analysis of the N-word, states it did not initially carry the extreme negative connotations it carries today; rather it had a benign meaning that defined blacks as childlike. This, to be sure, was belittling, but the term was not yet laden with animosity. By the 1800s the term had acquired strident negativity. "Nigger" meant that African Americans were infrahuman, a biologically inferior species of humans, and this was used to justify their enslavement. In other words, their race was being socially constructed in a negative manner. In the early years of slavery, according to Rahman, African Americans likewise used "nigger" as an identifier. For purposes of control, plantation owners did not buy all their slaves from the same tribe in Africa. They deliberately purchased slaves from different tribes on the premise that if they could not speak with each other it would be more difficult for them to organize and resist. Newly purchased slaves therefore underwent a period of adjustment in acquiring English. They learned that whites referred to them as niggers, and over time, they adopted the term as a common self-referent because it superseded tribal differences. However, many of their indigenous dialects did not emphasize the letter 'r' when it was the last letter of a word, and their pronunciation was "nigga" as opposed to nigger. Eventually nigga came to represent notions of solidarity and survival and it became a term of endearment. Today, African American males continue to use nigga to evoke solidarity in the same manner they use "brother" to address each other. The term has recently crossed racial boundaries and become more widespread in usage, due in part to the musical lexicon of the hip-hop generation, but some African Americans oppose its use (Asim 2007). They feel it is a symbol of their enslavement and an expression of self-hatred regardless of its spelling, and that it gives license to others to use the term "because they do." Others disagree and argue that the term should live as a reminder of their history and struggles, but they push back against other races using the term. They believe only they can cleanse this variation of the N-word of its negative and hostility-laden history. Hence the term is off-limits to others. Non-African Americans who use the term say they do so in solidarity with African Americans and their struggles.

Prejudice

At JB's the patrons' microaggressions included the use of nigger and nigga, but nigger was by far the more common term. Further, when the patrons did use "nigga" it was not in solidarity with African Americans but rather an expression of ill will. They did not hide their sentiments, nor were their racial utterances slips of the tongue that reflected unconscious racial animosity. As a social space of play and backstage area, the conventional norms of behavior in JB's were relaxed. There was little if any trepidation in using the term given that few if any African Americans were present for any length of time and the lack of normative prohibitions.

Soft Hostility

Expressions of prejudice in the bar, however, were more than just an attitude of ill will. They involved behavior and emotions as well. Behavior refers to the body language and the tone of utterances while emotions refer to the sensations people feel physically and subjectively during their behavior. Sometimes the patrons used the N-word in a normal tone of voice, with little animation, as a matter of fact, and in a calm and low-energy demeanor. This illustrated how normal their use of the N-word had become and what it represented. It reflected the internalization of an embedded and negative belief system that was part of their day-to-day lives. I refer to this regular usage of the N-word as "soft hostility," meaning that although it revealed disdain, it was devoid of displays of intense emotions and behavior. It was simply acceptable to use the N-word and all it implied. Examples of this normalcy follow.

> Mike is talking about a fellow coworker. He describes him as a "pretty good nigger."
>
> Mr. Jim is watching the news on television and says, "Sunday is nigger day at the rodeo."
>
> Some patrons are discussing a singer from Houston who sings well. "Is she a nigger?" someone asks.
>
> Chris discusses his trip to New Orleans. "There were a lot of niggers there," he says, "but we had a good time."
>
> Kid walks in and says, "Some niggers had a wreck down the street."
>
> Leo talks about a job he once turned down because he did not "want to work like a nigger."

Again, these comments were part of the patrons' normal conversations and they did not carry a tone of contempt, though the term clearly implied it. Their use of the N-word was routine, matter-of-fact, and part of their day-to-day living. Their prejudice, in other words, was normal.

Intense Hostility

Prejudice stimulates different emotions depending on the target. Gays, for example, evoke feelings of disgust (Crawford, Inbar, and Maloney 2014), and people afflicted with AIDS trigger fears of contamination (Marshall, O'Keefe, and Gross Fisher 1990). The emotions most often experienced by people who are prejudiced against African Americans are anger, fear, resentment, and anxiety (Neuberg and Cottrell 2002). On several occasions when some of the patrons made brief comments about African Americans, they generated angry reactions from other patrons. Once, a patron walked in and said, "A nigger was killed during a robbery attempt at the pawnshop on Lawndale." Another patron quickly responded in an angry tone with a scowl on his face, "Good, the motherfucker got what he deserved." In another instance, a patron told a story about a black bus driver hitting a pedestrian and not stopping to help. The sharp reactions included "fucking niggers" and "you can't trust a nigger." On another occasion, in a discussion about Africans from Africa and African Americans, a patron said in an agitated tone, "A nigger is a nigger regardless of where he's from." Tightened body and facial expressions accompanied these angry group expressions.

Anger, however, was not the only emotion triggered by the comments about African Americans. The feel-good emotions of laughter and superiority were also expressed when African Americans were the butt of jokes and ridicule (Buckley 2005). On one occasion, a patron drew laughter when he referred to a Chinese basketball player as a "Chinese nigger" because he was so tall. Also, at times, a single comment could trigger comments from other patrons. During a domino game, for example, the players were discussing Martin Luther King Day and whether they had the day off. One patron said that his company gave them a choice between Martin Luther King Day and Christmas. Everyone laughed. This stimulated another patron who chimed in that he could only take a half day off because he was only half-black. Everyone laughed again. Other times a single comment led to a larger group of patrons being motivated to join in the glee. The following mini-drama occurred on a Monday afternoon. Nine patrons were present and six participated in making comments. It began when Manuel, the only white patron present, asked me a question about the Houston Texans, the city's new professional football team. The Texans had played their first regular season opener in their new stadium the day before. Manuel and I were sitting on opposite ends of the bar and everyone heard our exchange.

"Did you go to the game?" Manuel asks me. "Yes, I did," I respond. "Did it cost you a lot?" he continued. "Well it was not cheap," I reply. "I am not ever going to contribute to those goddamn millionaire niggers," he responds in an agitated and forceful manner. There is laughter. "Oh man," Big Daddy leans over and tells me, "the shit is going to get hot." Gilbert walks in. "There is one of them now," Kid says to laughter. "I am one of what?" Gilbert asks as he approaches the bar. "You're a fucking nigger," Efren tells him from behind the bar. Everyone laughs. "Don't give me any of your shit," Gilbert angrily replies with force. "Hey, I didn't say you were a nigger, you asked what they said, and I told you," Efren responds. "Just give me a fucking beer," Gilbert says in an angry tone. "I was just telling everyone," Manuel tells Gilbert loudly, "that I would not give a fucking penny to attend one of the damn professional football games because all they are doing is screwing the common man with their outrageous prices. Six goddamn dollars for a beer and fucking outrageous ticket prices—hell, a poor man can't afford to take himself to one of those fucking games much less his kids. I wouldn't give a fuck if any of those teams never play another game, they're nothing more than a bunch of goddamn million-aire niggers, they piss me off. Did you read about Shawn Kemp [a profes-sional basketball player]?" he asks, waving an arm in the air. "They fired him from his 46-million-dollar job. Now he is going to have to live on two million dollars a year." "Damn that's tough," Big Daddy says sarcastically, "and now they want reparations for slavery. It used to be they wanted 40 acres and a mule, now they want 40 acres and a Cadillac." Everyone laughs. "You know," Gilbert says loudly, "people have always asked if God is black or white—well God must be white." "Why is that? Kid asks. "Because a nigger is never going to give up a rib," Gilbert replies. Everyone laughs, and someone begins to sing, "Free at last, free at last, thank God almighty I'm free at last," and several patrons join in. Everyone keeps laughing.

Manuel's anger-infused comments stimulated other patrons to express their negative opinions and join in the scapegoating, and their comments built upon each other in succession, especially after Gilbert's exchanges with Efren. The patrons had a common target and they were conforming to and reproducing the group's values. Under these circumstances, individuals feel extended into and part of the group (Allport 1954; Walker, Sinclair, and MacArthur 2015). Pleasure and cohesion were obtained through jokingly disparaging a group that was not like them (Hodson, Rush, and MacInnis, 2010).

The N-word as Insult

The N-word can also insult those who are not African Americans. To call someone the N-word is to impose upon the target the negative and dehumanizing characteristics associated with the term. When the name-calling occurs before a group, the reaction from the target has the potential to create conflict, as Gilbert's reaction illustrated. The patrons laughed when Efren called him the N-word, and though Gilbert responded quickly and angrily, he quickly summarized the situation and participated in the group's expression of negative sentiments.

What follows are three examples of the N-word being used to insult a non-African American. The first example is a story told by Willie to make a point about African Americans always complaining about being victims, but his story involved a white person who was the target of the N-word. The second example concerned John, who questioned if calling someone who was not an African American the N-word was offensive. He seemed to think not. The third example involved Big Daddy and his desire to change his nickname because he felt it had become associated with African Americans.

Willie

One afternoon as Willie was starting to leave the bar, he turned around quickly and engaged me.

"You know I want to ask you something—why is it that blacks always use racism as an excuse every time they get in trouble over something? When I got in trouble at work, I did not go around saying that people were after me because I was a Mexican." "Why did you get in trouble?" I ask. "For calling someone a nigger," he says. "Was it a black person?" I ask. "No, it was a white lady; she was not working very well, and I told her she had better step it up and she didn't, so I told her she was working like a nigger and she reported me. My boss told me that I had to go over to headquarters and see the manager and give him my side of the story and said I was in for a surprise. When I asked what he meant, he said 'you'll see.' Well, when I got to the manager's office, I opened the door and saw that he was black, and right away I told him, "Well I guess I lost this one." He smiled and said, "No, no you have not lost anything; sit down and tell me what happened." So, I sat down and told him everything, I didn't deny anything. He told me that he had reviewed my record and that I was a good employee who had done a lot for the company but that he could not overlook the incident. He said that I had a lot of vacation time coming so why didn't I take some vacation time, so I wouldn't lose any pay, and that's what I did, but I didn't start telling him that they were after me because I was a Mexicano." "Maybe," I respond, "African Americans have experienced so much discrimination that at times it is impossible to be objective about a situation." "Yeah, but we don't do that," he says.

When Willie called the white woman the N-word, it placed her in a stereotypical category that implied among other things that she was lazy and a slacker. Obviously, she felt demeaned and offended and thus reported Willie to the supervisor. It illustrated the power of the N-word to injure and anger regardless of the race of the target. What was not clear is why this incident triggered Willie's thoughts about African Americans always alleging discrimination. Perhaps he felt the white woman had reported him because he was a Mexican and that perhaps he should pursue this idea. Maybe he decided against it because he felt he would be "acting like a nigger." If true, it highlighted what the white woman and Willie may have had in common—a feeling of degradation when it involved the application of the N-word to one's persona. Willie's sentiments, of course, are speculation, but it may help explain why he asked me the question. He wanted to know why African Americans always alleged discrimination, but the incident that landed him in trouble did not involve calling an African American the N-word. An African American nevertheless played an important role in the incident. When Willie realized his manager was an African American, he believed he had little chance of getting a fair hearing. Willie anticipated the manager would be offended because of his use of the N-word. The opposite occurred. The manager put Willie at ease, listened to his explanation, and complimented him on his work for the company. He also told him he could not overlook the incident and suggested that Willie take the vacation time that he had accumulated so he would not lose any pay for the time he was going to be suspended. Willie agreed and said the manager had treated him fairly. Yet it did not occur to him that the manager might have been an example of an African American who did not feel persecuted because he was black, and who exhibited fairness in his assessments. Willie apparently had a blind spot that prevented him from altering his stereotype of African Americans always playing the race card. Blind spots concerning perceptions of African Americans are a common phenomenon (Krysan and Bader 2009). Further, Willie's assertions about Mexicans never alleging discrimination was not true. Many legal cases have gone to court alleging discrimination against Mexicans in the areas of civil rights, education, and employment.

John

In the next example, John implied that the N-word only stung when applied to African Americans. In this view, the white woman in Willie's story would not have any standing to complain. One afternoon John approached me as I stood at the bar talking with Harvey.

"I want to ask you a question, Professor," he tells me. "You too, Harvey, I would like your opinion. A friend of mine is in a bunch of shit because of what he said and I'm telling you they are getting all over his ass." "Who are you talking about?" Harvey asks. "Someone you know or someone in your department?" "He's not in my department but he's in my area. It's that justice of the peace who was calling a prisoner a nigger and they got him on film and now they are going after his ass. The funny part about the whole thing is that the person he called a nigger was not a nigger." "Was he a white prisoner?" I ask. "Yeah," John replies, "so my question to you is what does the dictionary say about who is a nigger and if it is a bad word?" His question surprises me. "I don't know exactly how the dictionary defines the term, but I'm sure that it says that it is an offensive term and that it is one of the most loaded words in race relations," I respond. "Well, you should know," he replies, "because you are at the university." He then leans in a little closer and again says in a lower tone of voice, "But the person he was cursing was not even a nigger; I tell you everybody in society is a victim." "Tell me about it," Harvey says.

It was surprising to hear John ask if the N-word was an offensive term and even more surprising when he implied it only carried negative connotations when it was applied to African Americans. He seemed to think only African Americans could be "niggers" and therefore when the term was applied to non-African Americans it did not carry an offensive meaning. It had no stinging value. He could not understand how a white person calling another white person a nigger was insulting, and thus he did not think the justice of the peace should have been in trouble. The justice of the peace, however, was in trouble, because the power of the N-word to demean was potent even when applied to a white prisoner, a person already labeled a deviant.

Big Daddy's Name Change

Big Daddy and JB had known each other for most of their lives. He was a regular customer and knew most, if not all the patrons. Big Daddy kept up with current events, especially politics, and one of his constant refrains was that African Americans had more power than Mexicans and only looked out for their own interests. In the following scenario, it was clear he felt passionate about the issue. His frustration increased as he vented about the lack of political power among Mexicans and his perceptions that the white power structure feared rioting among African Americans and that Mexican elected officials were not doing anything to change the situation. Big Daddy's fulminations began one afternoon a few moments after I walked into the bar. I greeted everyone and stood next to Big Daddy at the bar, and as we were shaking hands, he began the conversation.

"Did you see the article in the *Chronicle*?" he asks. "The one about Metro?" I ask. "Yeah," he says, "did you read it?" I nod my head yes. "I tell you, Professor, those damn blacks have more than their share of the pie and there it was, spelled out for all Houston to read. What more evidence does a person need?" he asks in an exasperated tone. "What was it, over 60 percent of the jobs at Metro were held by blacks while they are only about 25 percent of the population, and us? What are we, 40 percent of the population but have only 14 percent of the jobs? That's bullshit, Professor, and I know you know it is, but what I want to know is what are we going to do about it? I didn't hear Carol, Rick, Mario, or Sylvia [local Mexican elected officials] say anything, and what about Mayor Bill White? They all supported him for mayor, now will they go to him and ask him to do something about it, and will he do it or will he fear the blacks like most of those white boys? I tell you, Professor, we need to imitate the blacks and scare the hell out of those white folks just like they do; hell, why don't we threaten to burn and riot just like they do? I tell you, Professor, we are just too nice or scared or something to do anything. I don't understand it. What do you think?" "Well I think blacks have a lot of political influence and get the rewards because they deliver the votes," I respond. "That's what I'm talking about," Big Daddy exclaims loudly. "Until we do what they do, we will be left out. Hell, look at old Lee P. Brown [former African American mayor]. What did he do for us, nothing! I tell you, Professor, I think you ought to research how many more blacks started working in city government after Lee P. became mayor, and I know you will find that he did everything he could for them but did not do a goddamn thing for us. Hell, I would not be surprised if we lost ground." "Damn," Manuel says from the domino table, "you feel strongly about that shit." "Yeah, Big Daddy," JB chimes in from behind the bar, "don't hold back, tell us how you really feel." Everyone, including Big Daddy, laughs. "Hell, you know a black ain't going to do anything for us Meskins," Big Daddy responds. He laughs again as he takes a drink of his beer.

After thirty years, Johnny no longer wanted to be called Big Daddy. His real name was Johnny, but years ago, he developed the habit of calling all his male friends Big Daddy, and over time everyone began using the moniker to refer to his persona and it stuck. His desire to discard it caught the patrons by surprise and generated comment.

"Big Daddy doesn't want to be called Big Daddy anymore," JB says during a domino game. "Why?" Leo asks. "Because he says there too many niggers calling themselves Big Daddy," JB responds. Everyone laughs. "What does he want to be called?" Manuel asks. "I don't know," JB says. "He is going to have a hard time getting people to stop calling him Big Daddy," Leo chimes in. "I know," JB says, "he has been Big Daddy for a long time."

A few days later, the conversation again turned to Big Daddy wanting to drop his nickname. JB again reiterated the reasons and announced that Johnny Longneck was now his new moniker. "Johnny Longneck," several patrons said in unison while chuckling and laughing. The patrons asked how he came up with the name, but JB said he did not know. Several days later Johnny walked in and everyone greeted him as Big Daddy.

"I'm not Big Daddy anymore, gentlemen," he says, "it's Johnny Longneck." We smile. "Why don't you want to be called Big Daddy anymore?" Leo asks. "Because there are too many niggers who are calling themselves Big Daddy and I don't want to be confused with them. So now it's Johnny Longneck, gentlemen, Juanito Pesqueso Largo." Everyone laughs. "JB," he continues "give the boys a bucket, it's on Johnny Longneck." Everyone laughs again.

Johnny believed "Big Daddy" had become a black nickname and therefore he did not want the stigma he felt it conveyed. It was not clear how he arrived at this conclusion, but obviously he believed that it had become a disadvantage. Perhaps he felt that people would begin to wonder why he carried an African American nickname and conclude he had a strong association with them or that perhaps he had some African heritage. It was unlikely that the patrons would have thought this, but perhaps he was thinking of the public outside the bar. Regardless, it was clear that he was trying to shed his Big Daddy nickname and put Johnny Longneck in its place. He still wanted a nickname, but not Big Daddy because of his perception that it had become a "nigger" nickname. A few of the patrons did indeed start calling him Johnny Longneck or Johnny Long, but most continued to call him Big Daddy and Johnny eventually stopped correcting those who did, and over time the matter faded from conversation. Again, as in the previous two examples, this illustrated the power of the N-word but in an indirect manner, but it was enough to stimulate Big Daddy's desire for a name change.

Political Correctness and Manuel

Manuel was an old-fashioned racist and, perhaps, the bar's most vociferous critic of African Americans, so much so that on a few occasions White Mike told him that he would make a "good KKK member." Manuel's disparagement of African Americans emphasized that they were thieves, but he also repeatedly expressed resentment over the high salaries of professional athletes who were African Americans. Patrons said his antipathy was due to his business dealings with African Americans. Manuel bought cars at auctions and consigned them to car lots operated by African Americans and some never paid him when they sold his cars. These circumstances, however, only reinforced his negative views. One evening he stated that he had been using the term "nigger" for most of his life, thus indicating that his prejudiced views were of long standing, his business dealings notwithstanding. Yet, despite his negative sentiments and flawed business experiences, he continued to consign cars to their lots. His desire for profits trumped his prejudiced views, a common arrangement among those who do business with African Americans (Satter 2009; Lipsitz 2006).

One evening an exchange with Manuel resulted in my being labeled "politically correct." The modern origins of the phrase, politically correct, are in the Communist Party of the 1950s (Kohl 1992). If Party members strayed from the Party's official positions on the issues, they were not being politically correct in their interpretations and hence were criticized, and sometimes banned from the Party. The term therefore became associated with dogma. Today the phrase is used to ridicule those who insist upon language that does not disparage categories of people who are marginalized and disadvantaged. This is especially true of people who are of the conservative persuasion. While many people agreed with these sentiments, the critics maintained that the effort to cleanse the language had gone too far and impinged upon free speech. Further, and relevant to my situation, universities were viewed by some of the patrons as the bastions of political correctness because their speech codes prohibited any speech that insulted, stereotyped, or generally disparaged groups of people (Gould 2005). The critics alleged that offensive ideas required discussion without fear, and they mocked the adherents and advocates of political correctness as the "thought police" (Bruce 2001).

I acquired the label during a group discussion of the Texans, the city's professional football team. Manuel was engaging in his pet peeve and favorite harangue about the high salaries of African American football players. He repeatedly used the N-word as he ranted about "high dollar niggers" running up and down the football field. All the patrons in the bar were focused upon his performance. His anger was apparent, and his harangue lasted about forty-five seconds. When he paused for a moment I instinctively chimed in, "African Americans, Manuel, they are African Americans." He looked at me for a moment and then said, "I know, I know, you're right, Africo American is now part of being a nigger." Everyone laughed heartily and someone behind me said, "A nigger by any other name is still a nigger."

Other patrons had already noted my use of the term African American. Once, for example, when I used the term, a patron leaned over and said, "You say African American, but I say nigger." A few other patrons made similar comments. No one, however, had called me politically correct until my interactions with Manuel. From that moment on, whenever I was present the patrons began prefacing or following their use of the N-word by saying, "The Professor is politically correct and doesn't like the term" or "I know you call them African Americans" or "I know I'm not supposed to say this because it's not politically correct." They also attributed my political correctness to my affiliation with the University of Houston, as the following illustrates.

> The Canal Street door opens and White Mike walks in. "Damn," he says, "you can't sit outside because that nigger is painting, and the wind is blowing the paint over here. It is against the law to paint outside, but the nigger is doing it anyway. You know who I'm talking about, don't you?" he asks me as he sits down. "The African American across the street," I respond. "No," Mike quickly replies, "I mean that *pinche mayate*," he laughs and then continues, "I tell you the Professor is so damn politically correct." "He has to be," Chris interjects, "he can't be calling his students niggers, he has to be politically correct." "They're not niggers," Mike answers, "they are *pinche mayates*." He laughs again.

A *mayate* is a black bug in Mexico that moves slowly and without purpose and is used to refer to African Americans. It was not surprising, therefore, that the Mexican patrons used the term and that some white patrons like Manuel and White Mike had learned the term as patrons of a Mexican bar. *Pinche* can mean several things depending upon the context, e.g., unfair or stingy. Coupled with *mayate*, Mike used the terms to mean that "damn nigger" or perhaps something stronger.

On another occasion, we were playing dominoes, and several times during the game when someone made a good move Pinky chimed in with "nigger please" or "nigga please." After one such utterance, he said, "I know the Professor doesn't like for me to use the word nigger."

"How do you know?" I ask. "Because you are politically correct and teach race relations and I cannot imagine you condoning the word," Pinky replies. "He wants you to use African nigger," Manuel chimes in, to laughter. "You're not supposed to say that," Pinky responds. "I know, I know," Manuel says, "but a nigger is a nigger regardless if he is from Africa."

Just Kidding

I came to regret my interfering with Manuel's use of the N-word. It quickly became obvious that he deliberately used the term when I was present and enjoyed it. I violated the convention of ethnographic research of not saying or doing anything that deliberately altered the phenomenon one was there to observe and record. Ethnographers were not supposed to become part of the story. I had violated the rule and became a stimulus for Manuel's deliberate use of the N-word. He purposely played his racist role more times than he would have had I not corrected him. Manuel enjoyed teasing me by using the N-word while simultaneously conveying that he held me in affection. He would make a racist comment or deliberately mangle the term African American and then end his remarks by telling me that he was just joking, coupled with affectionate body language such as smiles, winks, touching my arm, and making remarks such as "I'm just kidding." These gestures conveyed, "I like you." Consider the following examples.

I am standing at the bar with Manuel, White Mike, and Efren. "Did you work today?" Manuel asks me. "Yes, but I left early," I respond. "What happened," he continues, "did you run out of *mayates* to teach?" Everyone laughs. "You know I'm just fucking with you," he says touching my arm and smiling. Several patrons shake their heads while also smiling.

During a domino game, I notice that Manuel's truck keys have a tag that used cars have when they are on car lots. "Are you selling your truck?" I ask. "Not the one you are thinking of," he replies. "This is another one. I think a nigger is going to buy it." He looks at JB and says, "Tatcho doesn't like me to use the word nigger; what word is it that you use?" he asks, "Africo nigger?" He laughs along with the others and then touches my arm and says, "I'm just putting you on."

The conversation turns to football and the Dallas Cowboys. "They need a new nigger quarterback," Manuel says. Everyone laughs. Manuel smiles and looks at me. "I know you don't like me to use that word," he says, "I should say, what is it, Africo ..." "African American," White Mike interjects. "Yeah that's it," Manuel responds, "that's what they need, a new Africo quarterback." Everyone laughs. Manuel looks at me, smiles, and winks.

We are standing at the bar talking about gambling. "Have you ever played Moon?" Manuel asks me. "No, and I never played dominoes until I started coming here," I respond. "Well," Manuel continues, "JB and I have been around bars most of our lives and that's where a lot of dominoes are played, and I drove a truck for 20 years and that's what truck drivers do when they get a break, play dominoes. So, while we were playing dominoes all those years you were at the college teaching niggers." Everyone laughs. Manuel looks at me, smiles, and says in a friendly manner, "You know I'm just messing with you."

Serious Manuel

On more than one occasion, Manuel engaged me in serious conversations about African Americans at the university. He asked how many I worked with, if they took my classes, whether I got along with them, and if they earned good grades. Often these conversations dealt with football, and Manuel frequently contended that African Americans did not possess the intelligence to play quarterback. "They don't have it up here," he would say while tapping his temple. His most frequent criticism was that African

Americans were thieves, and he gave examples from his car dealings. He spoke with anger and said they could not be trusted. One late afternoon after asking me several questions about African Americans at the university, Manuel once again said that in his opinion they were thieves. His tone was serious, and it was the only time I ever heard him use the phrase "African American," illustrating that he deliberately used "Africo" not only to tease me but to generate laughter as well. Leo was the only patron present when the following exchange took place and he engaged in stereotyping.

"Now the ones you work with may be okay," Manuel tells me, "but most them are nothing but a bunch of thieves and they will steal you blind." "How do you know this?" I ask. "Because I learned through my business that a nigger will steal you blind. Every time I put a machine [8 Liner] in one of their places, they would steal from me, and you know what they would tell me? That they accidentally left the door unlocked or that someone broke into the machines. Niggers are liars as well as thieves, and you know what, they train their children early. I was in a bar once and a nigger woman came in with her son and the first thing that kid did was run over to the jukebox and check the money slot. I tell you they train them to be thieves and they start them early." "How about the ones you do business with now?" Leo asks. "Same thing," Manuel replies. "They would steal from me in a minute if I didn't watch them." I listen quietly. "You don't agree, do you?" he asks. "Well I'm not going to say that there aren't black thieves, but there are thieves in every group, and I don't think all blacks are thieves. All groups have their good and bad, but most people are good." "Yeah you can say that, but you can't trust a nigger, I don't care how well educated he may be. I know you don't call them niggers, what do you call them, Africo . . ." "African Americans," Leo interjects. "Yeah, African Americans," Manuel says, "but those you work with treat you okay, you trust them?" "I have never had any problems," I respond. "How about you Leo?" Manuel asks. "About 55 to 60 percent of my union members are African Americans," Leo responds "and while they may give me a hard time on some of my stands, I don't have any problems with them. They sometimes think that I favor the Hispanic members, but hell the Hispanics think I favor the blacks." "Well, in my experience with them, and I've had a lot, I've learned that they are nothing but a bunch of goddamn thieves," Manuel replies.

In one instance, Manuel hired an attorney, filed suit, and eventually found the man who absconded with his cars. He brought the matter up during a domino game.

"Well," Manuel says, "they found my nigger." Everyone laughs. "Your nigger?" JB asks. "Yeah, he's in jail," Manuel responds. "Is he the one who owed you money?" JB asks. "Yeah, we're going to court soon," Manuel responds. "It has taken us two years, but we got the son of a bitch. We went to the Sheriff's Department and put out a warrant for his arrest and they found him just like that," he says, snapping his fingers. "I mean it took just a couple of days," Manuel explains. "Where did they find him?" I ask. "In jail. They had him for DWI and possession and now he has me on his ass," he answers. "How much money is involved?" JB asks. "Oh, about $80,000. He had five of my cars," Manuel replies. "Did you find out what happened to the cars?" JB asks. "I think he rented some, may have even sold one or two, but I'm not sure, all I know is they disappeared from his lot and then he disappeared. I tell you, can't trust a fucking nigger," Manuel responds.

Yet, despite his assertions of African Americans' inclination towards thievery, Manuel continued to place his cars on their lots, clearly indicating, as pointed out, that his quest for profits suppressed his prejudiced feelings (Lipsitz 2006). Manuel's claim that you could not "trust a nigger" was not borne out in the example below when he sounded contrite about his beliefs. A group of us were standing at the bar engaging in small talk when Manuel walked in and joined the conversation. After ordering a bucket of beer, he took a check out of his shirt pocket and showed it to everyone. It was for more than $8,000.

"Now how many times do you see a nigger give someone a check for over $8,000?" he asks. "You better hurry and take it to the bank," Leo says laughing, "he may not have good credit." Manuel laughs. "No, it's good," he responds, "it's a cashier's check, but how many times do you think a nigger has $8,000 in cash?" "Why did he give it to you?" Oscar asks. "He owes it to me for some of my cars he sold and that's not all he owes me. In fact, I was beginning to think that I would never see any part of it, but here it is." He pauses for a second. "I guess I shouldn't say too many bad things about them," he says in a soft voice, while laughing slightly.

Disapproval

Some patrons indicated their disapproval over the negative race talk about African Americans through their body language. They shook their heads in disagreement, raised their eyebrows and rolled their eyes, frowned, looked down, and covered their ears, often while they laughed. Many times, they glanced at me to gauge my reactions to negative remarks given I was perceived as politically correct. Some verbally expressed their displeasure by telling me, "it's hopeless, Professor" or "you can't teach them anything." Yet despite these signs of disapproval, only once was a serious objection observed. It occurred during a barbecue sponsored by the Vaqueros to raise scholarship funds. The bar was packed with men and women dressed in Western gear, and several of us, including the president of the Vaqueros, were standing at the bar talking. The race talk began when Manuel started commenting about his use of racial epithets during a Super Bowl party that he attended that was given by Jose.

"Man, I drank a lot of Crown," Manuel says. "Yeah, we know," Jose chimes in, "and you had a good time." "Yeah," Manuel responds. "I remember yelling 'run nigger run' at the television screen." "Do you remember your conversation with Big Al?" Jose asks. "Yeah, I remember telling him 'fix me a drink nigger, fix me a drink.'" Gilbert glances in my direction and Manuel touches me on the arm. "Now I know you want me to call them Africo Americans," he says, "but you know I'm too used to calling them niggers." Gilbert again glances at me. "You know," the president of the Vaqueros says, "they are celebrating this month, it's their month, Nigger

Heritage Month, and I was downtown, and they were having this parade and—" "A nigger parade," Manuel interjects." "Yeah, a nigger parade because this is their month," the president continues, "and—" IT'S AFRICAN AMERICAN HERITAGE MONTH," Eva shouts from the other end of the bar, "IT'S NOT NIGGER ANYTHING AND YOU SHOULD KNOW BETTER AND SHOW SOME RESPECT AND THINK ABOUT WHO YOU REPRESENT." Eva's comments catch everyone off guard and there are a few seconds of silence before the president breaks it. "That's what I'm saying," he continues without looking at Eva, "it's African American Heritage Month and they had this parade downtown, and we were stuck in the traffic, that's all I'm trying to say."

Eva walks out the Drennen Street door. Gilbert and I again exchange glances. After several moments of silence, Manuel leans over and speaks in a quiet voice.

"Hell, I've been called a Pollock all my life and that hasn't been easy either." "You can't use that term anymore," Gilbert says, "just like you can't use the term nigger." "I know, I know," Manuel replies, "but I've been using that word all my life and I can't seem to break the habit." He throws up his arm in resignation and continues while laughing, "I've also been a Mexican for about fifty years too and that hasn't been easy either." We laugh.

Eva's admonishment was an example of females exhibiting less prejudice towards African Americans in comparison to men, perhaps because of their experience in dealing with sexist attitudes and practices. They know how it feels to be the object of ridicule and disparagement because of their gender (Hoxter and Lester 1994). Gilbert and Manuel acknowledged the changed norm concerning the use of the N-word, but Manuel, though expressing awareness of the new standard, nevertheless called his use a habit that he could not break. He defended himself by declaring the strain he endured because of his twice-over minority status, "a Pollock" and a "Mexican and that hasn't been easy either." Manuel was referring to his Polish heritage and his long association with Mexicans and his intimate relations with Mexican women. This insight, however, did not make him sensitive to African Americans. The president of the Vaqueros was speaking in a normal, matter-of-fact tone when he uttered the N-word, and both he and Manuel illustrated their embedded prejudice in their repertoire of opinions and perceptions. Manuel even said that his use of the N-word was a habit that he could not break, implying how deeply embedded the word and its sentiments were in his psyche.

Conclusions

The use of the N-word served several functions for the patrons. It was used as a source of cohesion between the Mexican and white patrons. They coalesced into a larger group based on their shared views about African Americans. The N-word was also an expression of superiority. It meant that African Americans as human beings were less than the Mexican and white patrons. Thus, its use bolstered their self-esteem. It also released their anger and aggression. When an African American bus driver hit a pedestrian and failed to stop, the angry comments included "fucking niggers," and when a patron said an African American was shot during a robbery, the response was "good, the motherfucker got what he deserved." Likewise, its use served as a source of entertainment, as seen in the jokes that made the patrons laugh.

The patrons exaggerated their sentiments because they had group support. There were no sanctions in JB's for openly expressing negative comments about African Americans. Emphasis and exaggeration were group norms, and the patrons could be easily stimulated to express and overstate their opinions (Crandall, Eshleman, and O'Brien 2002). Also, it is difficult to question "group think." To question prejudice in the bar deviated from their norms and no doubt would have caught the attention of the other patrons and would have served as stimulus for comment, as my situation illustrated. Indeed, the literature indicated that the desire to be accepted was prominent and this acted as a deterrent to going against group norms, even if one did not agree with what was being said (Allport 1954). Also, JB's was a backstage social space, and it is in these areas where people make their true feelings known (Houts Picca and Feagin 2007).

Prejudiced feelings are variable and range from intense to mild, and not all the patrons expressed prejudice against African Americans, and a few gave indications of discomfort. Given, however, that negative sentiments about African Americans were endemic to American culture, it would have been surprising if any of the patrons—or any Americans, for that matter— were untinged by prejudiced feelings. Further it has been generally believed that younger cohorts, those born after World War II, were less prejudiced than older cohorts, those born before World War II, and while research has documented this to be the case (Wilson 1996) it must be understood that it is not an absolute generalization that applies to everyone in a cohort. The majority of JB's patrons, for example, were born in the 1940s and 1950s, and they still held prejudiced views towards African Americans.

Conclusion

Most Mexicans and whites in Houston live segregated from each other, but a significant number are integrated. They reside in the same neighborhoods, attend the same schools, are friends, date, marry, and divorce. The apex of social integration is intermarriage. One survey showed that 46 percent of Hispanics in Houston intermarried from 1960 to 1990, with a majority being with whites, and it is probable intermarriage will continue at a noticeable pace (Valdez 1997). In another survey, for example, conducted by the Kinder Institute of Houston, residents reported that 39 percent of Hispanics said they had been in a romantic relationship with a white person (Klineberg et al. 2014). In both surveys, people of Mexican origin made up most of the Hispanics.

The Mexican and white males who were JB's patrons were an example of social integration at the friendship level. The bar was the breeding ground for their commonalities and racial differences to mesh into friendships. The Mexicans and whites genuinely liked each other. Their mutual affection was obvious. They truly enjoyed each other's company and their aggressive but playful interactions. If this were not true, the same group of whites would not have been patrons of JB's for such a long period of time. Ongoing social interactions, however, do not necessarily lead to a dissipation of racial differences, as the race talk in the bar illustrated. Indeed, their racial differences were part of the bar's culture, but their friendship allowed them and their strains to surface and be dealt with. It did not tear their relationships asunder, but neither was race swept under the rug and ignored. Rather, it surfaced through humor, but not always. Some racial exchanges were tense and deliberate in tone and message, and in other instances, the targets of the racial jokes did not always laugh, but for the most part the patrons infused their racial comments and implications with frivolity, which everyone tacitly understood as "just joking." Thus, the patrons can be said to have a joking relationship. Joking allowed for a mutual form of permitted disrespect (Collinson 1988). It was the safety valve that allowed the various attacks that the patrons leveled at each other. The joking atmosphere was how the patrons funneled their humorous microaggressions and reproduced themselves as Mexicans and whites. As illustrated in the previous chapters, the overall pattern of their microaggressions was the Mexican patrons attacking the white patrons more than vice versa. The Mexican patrons were attacking the idea of white supremacy (Gibbons 2018) and white privilege (McIntosh 1989), the beliefs that whites were a superior race and as a result inherited unearned advantages and benefits by virtue of their skin color. In contrast Mexicans and African Americans inherited disadvantages because they were not white. Thus, the humorous microaggressions the Mexican patrons were leveling at the white patrons can be interpreted as resistance to white hegemony. Further, given that the white patrons tended to be the targets of the Mexican patrons' microaggressions more than vice versa, it is clear that an element of Mexican payback was involved. The Mexican patrons had more relative power because it was their bar in the Mexican part of town, and their numbers in the bar were greater relative to the white patrons. Payback refers to getting even and settling a score, of exacting revenge. There are an infinite number of reasons for seeking payback, e.g., rejection in a romantic relationship, being unjustly fired from a job, being the target of derogatory gossip, having one's honor publicly violated, being taken advantage of, etc. (Barreca 1995; Rosenbaum

2013). Most wronged people experience feelings of wanting to get even, but few ever act upon their feelings due to self-restraint or the lack of the opportunity to do so. The Mexican patrons, therefore, were opportunistic. The white patrons were always present and thus they became symbolic targets for the Mexicans, who experienced second-class status historically at the hands of white America. The Mexican patrons did not continually expound upon their personal encounters with white prejudice, but comments illustrated their awareness. Consider the following:

Frank mentions that the Mexicans called his elementary school *la esquela de piojos*—the school of lice—because the first thing the white teachers did when the Mexican kids arrived in the morning was check their hair for lice. It was embarrassing, and parents complained, but they were ignored, he said.

I once asked Mr. Charlie how he received his nickname and he made the following comment. "I used to be Jose, but when I was young my aunt told me I couldn't make it in the U.S. as Jose in those days, so I changed it."

A group of Mexican patrons are at the bar talking about growing up poor in Second Ward. "You knew the Anglos looked down on us," Kid says, "but to tell you the truth I had little contact with them, but you knew."

Gilbert tells a story about his mother going to his school and speaking to him in Spanish in front of his baseball coach. "He told her not to speak Spanish and to speak English, and you know what, he was a Mexican, but he spoke like a cowboy, you know with a country twang, but hell he was really white."

John says there are not any Mexican assistant police chiefs. "You hear all that stuff about brotherhood in the department," he says, "but when it comes down to it, they don't want any of us at the higher levels."

A group of patrons are talking about Mr. Charlie's hustling ways. "He's always been that way," Gilbert says. "He was the first one in the neighborhood who had a television set. Whites looked down on Mexicans because we didn't have anything, but Mr. Charlie had things other Mexicans didn't have. He had standing."

Wire says the police broke up their tailgating party at the end of the

Texans game last Sunday. "They were really aggressive and one constable right away calls for backup when he saw it was a group of Mexicans. 'We need back up,' he started saying out loud into his walkie-talkie, 'We need back up.' Man, something bad could have happened because some of the guys, you know, had been drinking and didn't like the way the guy was saying 'we need back up.' They came on too strong just because they saw a group of Mexicans drinking."

Realistically, Mexicans do not have to experience negative sentiments and treatment from whites to know that it exists. It is general knowledge among Mexicans and has long been part of the social environment, especially in Texas. As these words are being written, anti-Mexican sentiments are strident because of immigration, bilingual education, and the growing use of the Spanish language in public affairs. These issues have long sparked the ire of whites. Given this history, the white patrons in the bar became the symbols of the white oppressors and the targets of get-even sentiments. No doubt the Mexican patrons liked the white patrons, but this did not absolve them of the sins of white people, as was made obvious through their constant criticisms of whiteness. The most obvious examples were the way JB greeted White Mike, the Mexicans' superiority stances, their use of the phrase "white boy," and Efren's aggressive interactions with the white patrons. The Mexican patrons, however, did not seem aware of their payback feelings. I do not believe the Mexican patrons consciously said to themselves, "I'm going to JB's to get even with the white boys." Rather the microaggressions leveled against the white patrons seemed to be automatic, intuitive, and without forethought. They were instant, split-second, and immediate and reflected attitudes that existed outside of their realm of day-to-day consciousness, but were nevertheless stimulated into awareness by the continuous presence of the white patrons. The social psychology literature refers to these unconscious feelings as implicit attitudes because their existence cannot be directly determined (Greenwald and Banaji 1995). People are reluctant to admit that they hold negative attitudes about other racial groups, especially in public settings. Some do this deliberately, but others sincerely believe they are not prejudiced. Assessing unconscious-bias attitudes therefore requires indirect methods. This usually involves subjects matching descriptive words, such as nice, mean, dangerous, lazy, intelligent, etc., with the faces of different races, usually white and black faces, as fast as possible. The assumption is that subjects react to images automatically, that is, unconsciously. The results consistently showed that whites attributed more negative stereotypical attributes to African Americans than to white Americans. This was true even for people who tested low in prejudice and who were truly committed to racial equity. A major void in this research is how Mexicans unconsciously feel about whites, even though scholars have documented their resentments (De Leon 1983). The overwhelming emphasis, however, has been on the implicit attitudes of whites towards African Americans. Only two studies were found that dealt with the implicit attitudes of other minorities. One reported that Latinos, African Americans, and Asian Americans stereotyped whites as racist, arrogant, uncoordinated, ambitious, and intelligent (Conley, Rabinowitz, and Rabow 2010). The second study dealt with Mexicans in South Texas, and it reported that 23 percent held negative and stereotypical views about whites, but their sentiments were not described in detail (Fabiola and Gasquoine 2012). These studies suggested that the Mexican patrons' attitudes towards the white patrons were embedded in their unconscious.

The restraint exhibited by the white patrons' racial attacks leveled against the Mexican patrons were also intuitive. There was the occasional exception, as when a white patron told a Mexican patron to kiss his white behind, but this was a rare exception rather than the rule, and when the white patrons did engage in racial attacks, they were relatively mild. Obviously, their small numbers played a part. Had their numbers been greater, perhaps they would have been more strident in their comments and made them more often. This, however, was not the situation. The white patrons, therefore, were in a gray area of adherence. They could level critical attacks at the Mexican patrons and engage in disputes, but they could not assail in kind to what they experienced because of the social situation in which they found themselves as a small group of whites in a Mexican bar and the history of Mexican-white relations that impinged upon their presence. They seemed to understand this and thus accepted the sins of white people and white society because in the bar they had relatively less power. Under these circumstances, they seemed to be intuitively aware of an invisible boundary as to how far they could go with their microaggressions and their content. Though they ridiculed the notion of political correctness, they were nevertheless practicing their own version. The Mexican and white patrons were acting implicitly, with the Mexican patrons engaging in payback and the white patrons practicing their own version of political correctness.

Self-Identification

The race talk in the bar not only included the dialogue between the Mexican and white patrons but also the internal dialogue the Mexican patrons had among themselves. Though they thought of themselves as Mexicans, they were aware of the other labels the community had used to identify themselves to the broader white community. This identity dance was a consequence of Mexican-white relations in the broader society, where the noun Mexican had negative connotations. The community's response had been to use labels that avoided the term Mexican, such as Latin American, Chicano, Hispanic, and Latino. When the noun Mexican was used, it was as a modifier, as in the term Mexican American. The Hispanic label was scorned by some of JB's Mexican patrons, the only self-identifier to be so criticized. It was referred to as "Hispanic bullshit," "quacha," "that Hispanic mess," "that Hispanic stuff," and said to lack definition. "I don't know what the hell it means," a patron once observed. In a discussion over which racial group was doing the fighting in Vietnam, Leo declared with disdain, "It was us, Hispanics, or whatever the hell they were calling us." In another discussion on the same topic, Chris made the following comment in an emphatic tone, and he referenced three different identities in his short statement and likewise expressed disdain over the moniker Hispanic.

Who do you think was fighting in Vietnam? It was us and I'm setting Hispanic aside, I don't even like to use that damn term, it was us, Mexicans, Chicanos, that's who.

The question of Mexicans being white, raised by Mr. Charlie, speaks directly to the different color hues that are found among Mexican Americans. Skin tone affects the intensity and frequency of discrimination. The lighter the skin tones, the less discrimination Mexicans experience, with the very light-skinned being able to pass as white. Fair-skinned Mexicans also have better chances in life than the dark-skinned (Arce, Murguia, and Frisbee 1987). Specifically, the lighter the skin, the greater the chances of earning a better income (Telles and Murguia 1990), receiving a higher education (Murguia and Telles 1996), obtaining better housing (Alba, Logan, and Stults 2000), and experiencing better outcomes when interacting with the criminal justice system (Viglione, Hannon, and DeFina 2011) and when seeking employment (Espino and Franz 2002).

The study of the effect of whiteness upon the psyche and emotions among Mexicans is extensive, but usually not recognized as such because it operates under the label of acculturation and/or assimilation. These terms refer to the degree to which Mexicans and other Latinos acquire, borrow, and internalize the culture of white America. The acquisition of white culture includes everything from first names to dress, language, food consumed, place of residence, the ethnicity of close friends, and intermarriage. White Mexicans—that is, those who are thoroughly acculturated—are often ridiculed and called "pochos," "agringados," "agavachados," and "coconuts," meaning that they are more culturally white than Mexican. Leo once referred to a former girlfriend as "agavachada, but you know a good person, nevertheless." On another occasion, JB spoke of a Mexican male who became president of their bowling league. "It started going down," he said, "because he was agavachado and couldn't relate to Chicanos." One of the police officer patrons also spoke similarly of a Mexican officer assigned to patrol the Mexican neighborhoods. "He had never been around us, you know, but he took the assignment seriously and went out of his way to learn and did okay. You have to give him credit." William Madsen (1964), in his article on the agringado, points out that Mexicans in South Texas who were thoroughly acculturated into white culture often become alcoholics, but whether this was the case with the police officer mentioned by the patrons was unknown since it was not alluded to in their conversation.

Two major generalizations from the research about whiteness and Mexicans can be made. First, as previously stated, each succeeding generation in the United States becomes more culturally white in comparison to previous generations, and second, becoming white causes stress and anxiety especially for those who have dark skin. Thus, heavy drinking (Black and Markides 1993), drug use (Vega et al. 1998), depression (Codina and Montalvo 1994), loss of ethnic identity (Cuéllar et al. 1997), and feelings of alienation are not uncommon among the culturally white Mexicans (Michelson 2003). Heavy drinking and drug abuse also increases for acculturated Mexican women (Black and Markides 1993). Some of JB's Mexican patrons were acculturated, and heavy drinking occurred in the bar, but whether this was a function of acculturation, class position, gender, or a combination of these factors is not known. Nevertheless, were it not for immigration from Mexico, more American-born Mexicans raised in the United States would be more culturally white than is currently the case. Immigrants are agents of cultural transmission and they have kept Mexican culture alive and vibrant in Houston, but if their numbers dramatically decreased, the process of whitening among the Mexican population in Houston and the United States would, in all probability, rapidly increase, along with the associated social ills and gains.

Prejudice

The patrons' prejudiced attitudes towards African Americans raises the question of how it can be reduced. The research indicates that there are two ways, through contact and cohort replacement (Ryder 1965; Firebaugh and Davis 1988; Pettigrew and Tropp 2006). Contact between different races can lead to a reduction in prejudice because it facilitates familiarity, induces empathy, and reduces anxiety (Pettigrew and Tropp 2006, 2008). The ongoing friendship between the Mexican and white patrons was testimony to the validity of the contact thesis. The patrons, however, did not have extensive interaction with African Americans. Leo had the most contact in his duties as the president of a union, but he openly expressed hostility as well as acceptance towards African Americans. Also, it was not clear how extensive and intimate his contact was. It may have been cursory and perfunctory. Nevertheless, there was a hint of evidence in the bar that suggested that contact with African Americans could change attitudes. Big Al, for example, was well liked and accepted as an equal. He came to the bar with sponsors, that is, with Mexican patrons who were his friends. This facilitated his acceptance by the other patrons, Mexicans and whites alike. This added credence to the research findings that suggests that if a person from racial group A (Mexicans) has a friend from racial group B (African Americans) this facilitates B's acceptance by other members of group A (Aberson, Porter, and Gaffney 2008). Also, the contact between Big Al and the Mexican patrons occurred in an informal setting, a social space of play that allowed the patrons to get to know each other on an informal basis. Another example was Calvin, the African American boyfriend of Maria, a Mexican who visited the bar on Friday nights with a mixed group of white and Mexican employees from a nearby local company. Calvin was the only African American in the group and was obviously accepted by his peers and by the Mexican and white patrons in the bar, given that his group visited somewhat regularly on Friday evenings. Leo's interaction with Chuck, the African American proprietor of the manufacturing plant across the street from JB's, is also instructive. Recall that during their contact, Chuck gave Leo permission to use the N-word. This apparently impressed Leo, and he referred to Chuck as a "pretty good black guy." This meant that Leo felt like he could have an honest conversation with Chuck without worrying about saying something negative. Their interaction was informal, and it led to positive feelings on the part of Leo. JB also became involved in the incident. The next day when Chuck came to the bar to purchase a bottle of water, JB mentioned the conversation with Leo and stated somewhat apologetically, "Well the first thing you have to know about Leo is that he's crazy." JB was making sure that Chuck was not offended, and in doing so expressed empathy and concern as well as likability. There was also the example of Mike's description about a coworker as "a pretty good nigger." This likewise implied likability, but it was also an expression of ambivalence given that his normal use of the N-word illustrated soft hostility. There were also the frowns, the shaking of heads among some of the patrons that indicated a discomfort with the candid expressions of prejudice in the bar. Yet, these positive but very limited examples also occurred within the context of a social environment that also allowed and accepted prejudiced views. These expressions of negative feelings were normative and a prime example of JB's being a backstage area. There were no areas of the patrons' lives, however, where they would have informal contact with African Americans on a regular basis. Indeed, this is the situation for the overwhelming majority of Americans in the United States. Hence the opportunities for a lessening of negative feelings are not readily available.

The second method for reducing prejudice against African Americans is cohort replacement. This refers to younger, less prejudiced people replacing older, more biased people because of the higher mortality rates among the older generations. Several scholars believe this will lead to a reduction in prejudice. Welch and Sigelman (2011), for example, reported that the number of whites who viewed African Americans as hardworking and intelligent increased from 1992 to 2008. The increase occurred among people who were southerners, non-southerners, Democrats, Independents, Republicans, and among those who had high school degrees, some college, and college degrees. Other scholars have reported that opposition among whites to discrimination against blacks in home sales, intermarriage, and segregated schools declined from 1972 to 2008 (Bobo et al. 2012). Both studies relied upon cohort analysis. Other research, however, has suggested caution in accepting cohort declines in prejudice over time. Forman and Lewis (2015), for example, reported that racial apathy among white cohorts increased from the early 1990s to 2000. Also, at least one commentator speculated that Barack Obama's election as president led to a "whitelash" and the election of Donald Trump over Hillary Clinton in the presidential race of 2016. Whitelash refers to a feeling among whites that African Americans, Mexicans, and other nonwhites were taking over "their country" and hence reinforcing if not increasing prejudice sentiments (Boyd 2016; Lewis 2016). Most of the Mexican and white patrons were born in the 1940s and were in their twenties in the 1960s when restrictive racial norms affecting African Americans were seriously challenged and African Americans began making gains in dismantling them. If this was a result of a reduction in prejudice against African Americans, however, it did not occur among all Americans, as the patrons in the bar illustrated.

The End

As the research progressed, it became obvious that JB's was in the last stages of its career as a neighborhood bar. JB often talked of retiring and leasing or selling the bar, saying that he was tired and weary of being a bar owner. "It's provided me with a good living, and I have had a great time, but I'm tired and need to rest," he often said. By 2009, his business had slowed considerably, and he began closing the bar earlier. The afternoons continued to draw regular patrons, but even they were smaller in number. Among the white patrons, White Mike and his wife divorced, and he eventually stopped coming to the bar after being a regular patron for more than twenty years. He occasionally stopped by and had a beer, but he never stayed long. On one such visit, he relayed that he was now a patron of the Neon Moon Saloon, a bar located in La Porte, Texas, a few miles outside of Houston. Jerry and Mr. Jim both stopped drinking and no longer visited the bar. Jerry dropped by a few times, but no one had seen or heard from him in more than two years. Harvey fell late one evening while climbing the stairs to his apartment and incurred a serious head injury, and his convalescing kept him away from the bar for more than a year. The absence of white patrons meant that the Mexican-white race talk in the bar had all but ceased. Racial comments continued, but they were not as numerous and mostly directed towards African Americans. The absence of the white patrons made it clear that they stimulated the race talk in the bar by their presence.

Death had also taken its toll on JB's Mexican patrons. Mr. Charlie died suddenly on May 28, 2008, after having a door slammed on his hand at his home. He went to the hospital, where he went into shock, suffered a heart attack, and died. Several days later, Manuel died from cancer. His cancer had been in remission for a few years, but it returned, and over a period of several months it consumed his body and he passed. Mr. Charlie and Manuel were buried on the same day but at different cemeteries. For several days, we did not play dominoes as a gesture of respect to both, but especially for Mr. Charlie. JB leaned the chairs on the domino table and put a wreath in the center of the table. The day before their burials JB and several patrons toasted their lives and friendship with shots of tequila. Their lives and deaths were topics of conversation for several days. Everyone agreed that both Mr. Charlie and Manuel had lived full lives. Everyone spoke of Mr. Charlie's hustling life and mental and physical acuity until the very end of his ninety-three years. Likewise, Manuel's business acumen was acknowledged. "He knew how to make a dollar" and "he made a lot of money" were the sentiments expressed. Both Mr. Charlie and Manuel were said to have left their wives "well taken care of," especially Manuel. The domino players talked about how their deaths were going to affect the domino game, given that both were dedicated players. The general sentiment was that the patrons were "running out of players." I visited Manuel at the funeral home the day before his burial and attended Mr. Charlie's funeral the next day. Efren died in March of 2009. He smoked cigarettes for most of his adult life and developed lung cancer. He had not been a regular patron of the bar for more than a year before his death; he occasionally visited and played dominoes, but he was not his usual aggressive self. I did not immediately hear about his death and regret that I missed the funeral. Leo likewise stopped being a regular patron and started visiting the Tall Texan, a bar located in the Northside of Houston. I sought him out at his new watering hole and asked why he had stopped visiting JB's. "There's nothing going on there anymore," he replied, "the place is dying."

In June 2009, JB sold the bar to Tino, who became the new owner. Before JB turned the bar over to Tino, his business increased as patrons from the past and present came by to see if it was true that he had sold the bar. The weekend before Tino took possession, the patrons held a barbecue for JB, and there was a lot of reminiscing about the "good old days" and how the bar might change from this point on.

After the new owner took over, JB visited several times a week and played dominoes and acted like the regular patron he had become. Over time, however, he moved permanently to his beach house in Crystal Beach,

Texas, about sixty-five miles from Houston, and his visits became infrequent. He also moved some of his possessions from the bar, most significantly the jukebox. Tino installed a new computerized jukebox that was more expensive to play, and which the patrons found too complicated to navigate; plus, many of the old Tejano songs that the patrons had been playing since the bar opened were not available on the new machine. After two months Tino realized that the computerized jukebox was not being extensively played and he installed his own CD player, and the patrons began bringing their own music that they could play for free and the computerized jukebox was removed. When JB removed the table that sat a few feet in front of the bar, Tino replaced it with several tall, round tables that could sit up to four people. He also put more tables and chairs on the deck. For the most part Tino was an absent owner. The young women whom he employed at his family's bakery located on the north side of Houston operated the bar. As might be expected, the presence of females led to touching, flirting, and sexual comments by the patrons. The most significant change Tino wrought was the stopping of patrons retrieving their own beer from behind the bar. This longtime practice ceased immediately. Interestingly, Tino did not announce the change. Everyone seemed to know intuitively that the practice would end. Tino said that he intended to continue the traditions of the Christmas party and the Marines' Birthday. The weekly meat pot had earlier ceased to exist because Willie the butcher retired. One uncertainty was the Super Bowl pot. In 2009, the bar held its first annual Christmas party under Tino's ownership, and the thirty-plus people who attended were his largest crowd since he opened. Since Tino had taken over, business had seriously slumped. There were days when the domino players were the only patrons at the bar, and some evenings the bar closed early because no one or only one or two patrons were present. On the evening of November 2, 2010, Tino told Larry, a regular patron who was tending the bar, to close early, and that unfortunately his services would no longer be needed because the bar would not reopen. Tino said he was considering turning the bar into an eatery, and in September of 2017, he converted JB's into a taco house. Tino's decision to close the bar was not a surprise. The few patrons who remained talked about how slow business had become, but its suddenness nevertheless caught the few regular patrons of the bar by surprise. When Larry closed, he took the domino table to the D&W Lounge, another bar in the East End that catered to Mexican and white patrons. Some of the domino players and other patrons began visiting the D&W, and though it was an interesting place in its own right, it was three times the size of JB's and thus had neither the ambiance nor the group camaraderie that the patrons created and sustained through their interactions in JB's. It was simply too large to be duplicative. The community of men that were comprised by JB's is no more, except in the memories of JB and his patrons and on these pages where the last few years of this extraordinary drinking establishment were recorded. As Mr. Charlie would say, *Ya Estufas, It's Over.*

References

Aberson, Christopher L., Michael K. Porter, and Amber M. Gaffney. 2008. "Friendships Influence Hispanic Students' Implicit Attitudes towards White Non-Hispanics Relative to African Americans." *Hispanic Journal of Behavioral Sciences* 30, no. 4: 544–556.

Alba, Richard D., John R. Logan, and Brian J. Stults. 2000. "The Changing Neighborhood Contexts of the Immigrant Metropolis." *Social Forces* 79, no. 2: 587–621.

Allen, Irving Lewis. 1983. *The Language of Ethnic Conflict: Social Organization and Lexical Culture.* New York: Columbia University Press.

Allport, Gordon W. 1954. *The Nature of Prejudice.* Reading, MA: Addison-Wesley.

American Surnames. (n.d.). "What does the Name Meskin Mean?" https://www.names.org/n/meskin/about

Arce, C.H., E. Murguia, and W.P. Frisbee. 1987. "Phenotype and Life Chances among Chicanos." *Hispanic Journal of Behavioral Sciences* 9, no. 1: 19–22.

Asim, Jabai. 2007. *The N Word: Who Can Say It, Who Shouldn't and Why.* New York: Houghton Mifflin.

Atwood, Elmer B. 1962. *The Regional Vocabulary of Texas.* Austin: University of Texas Press.

Barreca, Regina. 1995. *Sweet Revenge.* New York: Harmony Books.

Bell, Michael J. 1983. *The World From Brown's Lounge.* Chicago: University of Illinois Press.

Benavidez, Roy, and John R. Craig. 2005. *Medal of Honor: One Man's Journey from Poverty and Prejudice.* Washington, DC: Potomac Books.

Black, Sandra A., and Kyriakos Markides. 1993. "Acculturation and Alcohol Consumption in Puerto Rican, Cuban American, and Mexican American Women in the United States." *American Journal of Public Health* 83, no. 6: 890–893.

Blanton, Carlos Kevin. 2000. "They Cannot Master Abstractions, but They Can Often Be Made Efficient Workers: Race and Class in the Intelligence Testing of Mexican Americans and African Americans in Texas during the 1920s." *Social Science Quarterly* 81, no. 4: 1014–1026.

Bobo, Lawrence D., Camille Z. Charles, Maria Krysan, and Alicia D. Simmons. 2012. "The Real Record on Racial Attitudes in Social Trends in American Life." In *Readings from the General Social Survey since 1972,* edited by Peter V. Marsden. Princeton, NJ: Princeton University Press.

Bonilla-Silva, Eduardo. 2006. *Racism without Racists: Color-Blind Racism and the Persistence of Racial Inequality in the United States.* Lanham, MD: Rowman & Littlefield.

Boyd, Herb. 2016. "White Backlash." *New York Amsterdam News,* November 10, 2016, 1.

Brodsky, Archie, and Stanton Peele. 1999. "Psychosocial Benefits of Moderate Alcohol Consumption: Alcohol's Role in a Broader Conception of Health and Well Being." In *Alcohol and Pleasure: A Health Perspective,* edited by Stanton Peele and Marcus Grant. Washington, DC: Taylor and Francis.

Bruce, Tammy. 2001. *The New Thought Police.* Roseville, CA: Prima Publishing.

Buchanan, Susy. 2005. "Tensions Mounting between Blacks and Latinos Nationwide." *Intelligence Report* (Summer), Southern Poverty Law Center, Montgomery, Alabama.

Buckley, F.H. 2005. *The Morality of Laughter.* Ann Arbor: University of Michigan Press.

Business Insider. 2018. Vol. 4.

Cantrell, Gregg. 2013. "'Our Very Pronounced Theory of Equal Rights for All': Race, Citizenship, and Populism in the South Texas Borderlands." *Journal of American History* 100, no. 3: 663–690.

Cavan, Sherri. 1966. *Liquor License: An Ethnography of Bar Behavior.* Chicago: Aldine.

Chacon Mendoza, Gustavo. 2008. "Gateway to Whiteness: Using the Census to Redefine and Reconfigure Hispanic/Latino Identity, in Efforts to Preserve a White American National Identity." 30 *U. La Verne L. Rev.*, 160-2008-2009.

Clark, Michael. 1970. "Humor and Incongruity." *Philosophy* 45, no. 171: 20-32.

Codina, Edward G., and Frank F. Montalvo. 1994. "Chicano Phenotype and Depression." *Hispanic Journal of Behavioral Sciences* 16, no. 3: 296-306.

Collinson, David L. 1988. "'Engineering Humor': Masculinity, Joking and Conflict in Shop-floor Relations." *Organizational Studies* 9, no. 2: 181-199.

Community Health Profiles, 1999-2003. City of Houston, Department of Health and Human Resources.

Conley, Terri D., Joshua Rabinowitz, and Jerome Rabow. 2010. "Gordon Gekkos, Frat Boys and Nice Guys: The Content Dimensions and Structural Determinants of Multiple Ethnic Groups' Stereotypes about White Men." *Analysis of Social Issues* 10, no. 1: 69-96.

Crandall, Christian S., Amy Eshleman, and Laurie O'Brien. 2002. "Social Norms and the Expression and Suppression of Prejudice: The Struggle for Internalization." *Journal of Personality and Social Psychology* 82, no. 3: 359-378.

Crawford, Jarret T., Yoel Inbar, and Victoria Maloney. 2014. "Disgust Sensitivity Selectivity Predicts Attitudes toward Groups That Threaten (or Uphold) Traditional Sexual Morality." *Personality and Individual Differences* 70 (November): 218-223.

Crosby, Faye J., and Cheryl Van DeVeer. 2000. *Sex, Race and Merit: Debating Affirmative Action in Education and Employment.* Ann Arbor: University of Michigan Press.

Cuéllar, Israel, Bill Nyberg, Roberto E. Maldonado, and Robert Roberts. 1997. "Ethnic Identity and Acculturation in a Young Adult Mexican-Origin Population." *Community Psychology* 25, no. 6: 535-549.

Davis, Murray S. 1993. *What's So Funny? The Comic Conception of Culture and Society.* Chicago: University of Chicago Press.

De Leon, Arnoldo. 1983. *They Called Them Greasers: Anglo Attitudes toward Mexicans in Texas, 1821-1900.* Austin: University of Texas Press.

De Leon, Arnoldo. 1986. *Ethnicity in the Sunbelt: A History of Mexican Americans in Houston.* College Station: Texas A&M Press.

De Leon, Arnoldo. 2000. "In Re Ricardo Richard: An Attempt at Chicano Disenfranchisement in San Antonio, 1896-1897." In *En Aquel Entonces (In Years Gone By): Readings in Mexican American History*, edited by Manuel G. Gonzales and Cynthia M. Gonzales. Bloomington: Indiana University Press.

De Leon, Arnoldo. 2001. *Ethnicity in the Sunbelt: Mexican Americans in Houston.* University of Houston Series in Mexican American Studies. Center for Mexican American Studies. College Station: Texas A&M Press.

Delgado, Richard, and Jean Stefancic. 2017. *Critical Race Theory.* New York: New York University Press.

Duncan, Brian, and Stephen Trejo. 2011. "Intermarriage and the Intergenerational Transmission of Ethnic Identity and Human Capital for Mexican Americans." *Journal of Labor Economics* 29, no. 2: 195-227.

Ely, Robert J., Debra E. Meyerson, and Martin N. Davidson. 2006. "Rethinking Political Correctness." *Harvard Business Review* 84, no. 9.

Espino, Rodolfo, and Michael M. Franz. 2002. "Latino Phenotypic Discrimination Revisited: The Impact of Skin Color on Occupational Status." *Social Science Quarterly* 83, no. 2: 612.

Fabiola Garza, Christelle, and Philip Gerard Gasquoine. 2012. "Implicit Race/Ethnic Prejudice in Mexican Americans." *Hispanic Journal of Behavioral Science* 35, no. 1: 121-183.

Felson, Richard B. 1978. "Aggression as Impression Management." *Social Psychology* 41, no. 3: 205-213.

Fernandez-Armesto, Felipe. 2001. *Food: A History.* London: Macmillan.

Fine, Gary Allen. 1983. "Sociological Approaches to the Study of Humor." In *Handbook of Humor Research,* vol. 1, *Basic Issues,* edited by Paul McGhee and Jeffrey H. Goldstein. New York: Springer-Verlag.

Firebaugh, Glen, and Kenneth E. Davis. 1988. "Trends in Antiblack Prejudice, 1972-1984: Region and Cohort Effects." *American Journal of Sociology* 94, no. 2: 251-272.

Flexner, Stuart Berg. 1976. *I Hear America Talking: An Illustrated History of American Words and Phrases.* New York: Simon and Schuster.

Forman, Tyrone, and Amanda Lewis (2015). "Beyond Prejudice? Young Whites Racial Attitudes in Post-Civil Rights America 1976-2000." *American Behavioral Scientist,* 59, no. 11: 1394-1428

Galvan, Roberto A., and Richard V. Teschner. 1995. *El Diccionario del Espanol Chicano: The Dictionary of Chicano Spanish.* Lincolnwood, IL: National Textbook Company.

Garcia, Ignacio M. 2009. *White but Not Equal: Mexican Americans, Jury Discrimination, and the Supreme Court.* Tucson: University of Arizona Press.

García, Juan Ramon. 1980. *Operation Wetback: The Mass Deportation of Mexican Undocumented Workers in 1954.* Westport, CT: Greenwood Press.

Geertz, Clifford. 1973. *The Interpretation of Cultures: Selected Essays.* New York: Basic Books.

Gibbons, Andrea. 2018. "The Five Refusals of White Supremacy." *American Journal of Economics and Sociology* 77, no. 3-4: 729-755.

Gilmore, David D. 1990. *Manhood in the Making: Cultural Concepts of Masculinity.* New Haven, CT: Yale University Press.

Glass, L.L. 1984. "Man's Man/Ladies' Man: Motifs of Hypermasculinity." *Psychiatry* 47, no. 3: 260-278.

Goffman, Erving. 1955. "On Face Work: An Analysis of Ritual Elements in Social Interaction." *Psychiatry: Journal for the Study of Interpersonal Processes* 18: 213-231.

Golding, Jacqueline M., Audrey M. Burnam, Bernadette Benjamin, and Kenneth B. Wells. 1992. "Reasons for Drinking, Alcohol Use, and Alcoholism among Mexican Americans and Non-Hispanic Whites." *Psychology of Addictive Behaviors* 5, no. 3: 155-167.

Goldman, Seth K. 2012. "Effects of 2008 Obama Presidential Campaign on White Racial Prejudice." *Public Opinion Quarterly* 76, no. 4: 663-687.

Gonzalez Reingle, Jennifer M., Raul Caetano, and Britain A. Mills, Patrice A. C. Vaeth. 2015. "Drinking Context and Companions as Predictors of Alcohol Use among Border and Non-Border Mexican Americans." *Hispanic Journal of Behavioral Sciences* 37, no. 1: 90-102.

Gould, Jon B. 2005. *Speak No Evil: The Triumph of Hate Speech Regulations.* Chicago: University of Chicago Press.

Graulich, Michel. 2000. *Aztec Human Sacrifice as Expiation.* Chicago: University of Chicago Press.

Green, Jonathon. 1998. *The Cassell Dictionary of Slang.* London: Cassell, 1998.

Greenwald, Anthony G., and Mahzarin R. Banaji. 1995. "Implicit Social Cognition: Attitudes, Self-Esteem, and Stereotypes." *Psychological Review* 102, no. 1: 4-27.

Guo, G., Y. Fu, H. Lee, T. Cai, K.M. Harris, and Y. Li. 2014. "Genetic Bio-Ancestry and Social Construction of Racial Classification in Social Surveys in the Contemporary United States." *Demography* 51: 141-172.

Hall, Peter, and Dee Ann Spencer Hall. 1983. "The Handshake as Interaction." *Semiotica* 45, no. 3/4: 249-264.

Heath, Dwight B. 2000. *Drinking Occasions: Comparative Perspectives on Alcohol and Culture.* Philadelphia: Brunner/Mazel.

Herrnstein, Richard J., and Charles Murray. 1994. *The Bell Curve.* New York: Free

Press.

Hill, Jane H. 2008. *The Everyday Language of White Racism*. Chichester, UK: Wiley-Blackwell.

Hodson, Gordon, Johnathan Rush, and Cara C. MacInnis. 2010. "A Joke Is Just a Joke (Except When It Isn't): Cavalier Humor Beliefs Facilitate the Expression of Group Dominance Motives." *Journal of Personality and Social Psychology* 99, no. 4: 660-682.

Houts Picca, Leslie, and Joe Feagin. 2007. *Two-Faced Racism: Whites in the Backstage and Frontstage*. New York: Routledge.

Hoxter, A. Lee, and David Lester. 1994. "Gender Differences in Prejudice." *Perceptual Motor Skills* 79: 1666.

Huizinga, J. 1949. *Homo Ludens*. Abingdon, UK: Routledge.

Infante, Dominic A., Bruce Riddle, Carl L. Horvath, and S.A. Tumlin. 1992. "Verbal Aggressiveness: Messages and Reasons." *Communication Quarterly* 40, no. 2 (Spring): 116-126.

Jackson, Marion and Joaquin Wilkinson. 2005. *One Ranger-A Memoir*. Austin: University of Texas Press.

Jay, Timothy. 1992. *Cursing in America*. Philadelphia: John Benjamin Publishing Co.

Jay, Timothy. 2000. *Social Theory of Speech*. Philadelphia: John Benjamin Publishing Co.

Kennedy, Randall. 2002. *Nigger: The Strange Career of a Troublesome Word*. New York: Pantheon Books.

Kimmel, Michael S. 2017. *Manhood in America: A Cultural History*. New York: Oxford University Press.

Klineberg, Stephen L. 2005. "The Houston Area Survey, 1982-2005: Public Perception in Remarkable Times." Figure 35, "Anglos Preferences Regarding the Racial Composition of Their Neighborhoods (1986-2005)." Houston: Kinder Institute, Rice University.

Klineberg, Stephen L., Jie Wu, Kira Douds, and Diane Ramirez. 2014. "Shared Prospects: Hispanics and the Future of Houston." Houston: Kinder Institute for Urban Research, Rice University.

Kohl, Herbert. 1992. "Uncommon Differences: On Political Correctness, Core Curriculum and Democracy in Education." *The Lion and the Unicorn* 16, no. 1: 1.

Korgen, Kathleen Odell. 2002. *Crossing the Racial Divide: Close Friendships between Black and White Americans*. Westport, CT: Praeger.

Kreneck, Thomas H. 2012. *Del Pueblo: A History of Houston's Hispanic Community*. College Station: Texas A&M Press.

Kriss Kross Directory. 1956. Houston: Wagner Kriss Kross Directory Co.

Krysan, Maria, and Michael D. Bader. 2009. "Racial Blind Spots: Black-White-Latino." *Social Problems* 56, no. 4: C1-C4.

Kuipers, Giselinde. 2008. "The Sociology of Humor." In *The Primer of Humor*, edited by Victor Raskin. New York: Mouton de Gruyer.

LeMasters, E.E. 1975. *Blue-Collar Aristocrats: Life-Styles at a Working-Class Tavern*. Madison: University of Wisconsin Press.

Lewis, Helen. 2016. "The Politics of Whitelash." *New Statesman*, November 11-17: 22-23.

Lipsitz, George. 2006. *The Possessive Investment in Whiteness: How White People Profit from Identity Politics*. Philadelphia: Temple University Press.

Lowe, Geoff, and Sharon B. Taylor. 1993. "Relationship between Laughter and Weekly Alcohol Consumption." *Psychological Reports* 72, no. 3: 1210.

Lowe, Geoff, and Sharon B. Taylor. 1997. "Effects of Alcohol on Responsive Laughter and Amusement." *Psychological Reports* 80, no. 3: 1149-1150.

Macrory, Boyd E. 1952. "The Tavern and the Community." *Quarterly Journal of Studies on Alcohol* 13, no. 4: 609-637.

Madsen, William. 1964. "The Alcoholic Agringado." *American Anthropologist* 66, no. 2: 355-360.

Marshall, Patricia A., Paul J. O'Keefe, and Susan Gross Fisher. 1990. "Touch and Contamination: Patients' Fear of AIDS." *Medical Anthropology Quarterly* 4, no. 1: 129-144.

Martinez, George A. 1997. "The Legal Construction of Race: Mexican Americans and Whiteness." *Harvard Latino Law Review* 2: 321-348.

Mass Observation. 1987. *The Pub and the People*. London: Cresset Library.

Matsuda, Mari J., Charles R. Lawrence III, Richard Delgado, and Kimberley Williams Crenshaw, eds. 1993. *Words That Wound: Critical Race Theory, Assaultive Speech, and the First Amendment*. Boulder, CO: Westview Press.

May, Reuben A. Buford. 2000. "Race Talk and Local Collective Memory among African American Men in a Neighborhood Tavern." *Qualitative Sociology* 23, no. 2: 201-214.

May, Reuben A. Buford. 2001. *Talking at Trena's: Everyday Conversations at an African American Tavern*. New York: New York University Press.

McIntosh, Peggy. 1989. "White Privilege: Unpacking the Invisible Knapsack." *Peace and Freedom Magazine* (July/August): 10-12.

McWilliams, Carey, and Matt Meier. 1990. *North from Mexico: The Spanish-Speaking People of the United States.* Westport, CT: Praeger Press.

"Meskin." (2011). *Urban Dictionary.* http://www.urbandictionary.com.

Michelson, Melissa R. 2003. "The Corrosive Effect of Acculturation: How Mexican Americans Lose Political Trust." *Social Science Quarterly* 84, no. 4: 918-933.

Middleton, Russell. 1959. "Negro and White Reaction to Racial Humor." *Sociometry* 22, no. 2: 175-188.

Mindiola, Tatcho, Jr., Yolanda Flores Niemann, and Nestor Rodriguez. 2002. *Black-Brown Relations and Stereotypes.* Austin: University of Texas Press.

Mirande, Alfredo. 1986. "Que Gaucho Ser Macho: It's a Drag to Be a Macho Man." *Aztlan: A Journal of Chicano Studies* 17, no. 2: 63-89.

Mirande, Alfredo. 1997. *Hombres y Machos: Masculinity and Latino Culture.* Boulder, CO: Westview Press.

Money, John. 1980. *Love and Love Sickness: The Science of Sex, Gender Difference, and Pair Bonding.* Baltimore: Johns Hopkins University Press.

Morin, Raul. 1966. *Among the Valiant.* Alhambra, CA: Borden Publishing Co.

Mosher, Donald L., and Silvan S. Tomkins. 1988. "Scripting the Macho Man: Hypermasculine Socialization and Enculturation." *Journal of Sex Research* 25, no. 1: 60-84.

Mosher, Donald L. 1991. "Macho Men, Machismo, and Sexuality." *Annual Review of Sex Research* 2, no. 1: 199-247.

Murguia, Edward, and Edward E. Telles. 1996. "Phenotype and Schooling among Mexican Americans." *Sociology of Education* 69, no. 4: 276-289.

Myers, Kristen. 2005. *Race Talk: Racism Hiding in Plain Sight.* Lanham, MD: Rowman & Littlefield.

Nericcio, William Anthony. 2007. *Tex[t]-Mex: Seductive Hallucinations of the "Mexican" in America.* Austin: University of Texas Press.

Neuberg, Steven L., and Catherine A. Cottrell. 2002. "Intergroup Emotions: A Biocultural Approach." In *From Prejudice to Intergroup Emotions,* edited by Diane M. Mackie and Eliot R. Smith. New York: Psychology Press.

Newitz, Annalee, and Matt Wray, eds. 1997. *White Trash: Race and Class in America.* New York: Routledge.

Newport, Frank. 2016. "Most in U.S. Oppose Colleges Using Race in Admissions."

Gallup Poll, June 29–July 2, 2016.

Oldenburg, Ray. 1989. *The Great Good Place: Cafes, Coffee Shops, Community Centers, Beauty Parlors, General Stores, Bars, Hangouts, and How They Get You through the Day*. New York: Paragon House.

Oliver, Mary Beth. 2003. "African American Men as Criminal and Dangerous: Implications of Media Portrayals of Crime on the Criminalization of African American Men." *Journal of African American Studies* 7, no. 2: 3–18.

Overmyer-Velazquez, Mark. 2013. "Good Neighbors and White Mexicans: Constructing Race and Nation on the Mexico-U.S. Border." *Journal of American Ethnic History* 33, no. 1: 5–34.

Pagliai, Valentina. 2010. "Introduction: Performing Disputes." *Journal of Linguistic Anthropology* 20, no. 1.

Panitz, Daniel R., Richard D. McConchie, S. Richard Sauber, and Julio A. Fonseca. 1983. "The Role of Machismo and the Hispanic Family in the Etiology and Treatment of Alcoholism in Hispanic American Males." *American Journal of Family Therapy* 11, no. 1: 31–44.

Paredes, Americo. 1961. "On Gringo, Greaser and Other Neighborly Names." In *Singers and Storytellers*, edited by Wilson M. Hudson, Mody C. Boatright, and Allen Maxwell, 285–289. Dallas: Southern Methodist University Press.

Paredes, Americo. 2003. "The United States, Mexico and Machismo." In *Perspectives on Las Americas: A Reader in Culture, History and Representation*, edited by Matthew C. Gutman, Felix Matos Rodriguez, Lynn Stephen, and Patricia Zavella. Oxford: Blackwell Publishing, Ltd.

Pawluk, C.J. 1989. "Social Construction of Teasing." *Journal for the Theory of Social Behavior* 19: 145–167.

Peele, S., and M. Grant, eds. 1999. *Alcohol and Pleasure: A Health Perspective*. Washington, DC: Taylor and Francis.

Pena, Manuel. 1985. *The Texas-Mexican Conjunto: History of a Working-Class Music*. Austin: University of Texas Press.

Perinbanayagam, R.S. 2000. *The Presence of Self*. Boston: Rowman & Littlefield.

Perlmutter, Philip. 2002. "Minority Group Prejudice." *Society* (March/April): 59–65.

Peterson, John H., Jr. 1975. "Black-White Joking Relationships among Newly-Integrated Faculty." *Integrated Education* 13, no. 1: 33–37.

Pettigrew, Thomas F., and Linda R. Tropp. 2006. "A Meta-analytic Test of Intergroup Contact Theory." *Journal of Personality and Social Psychology* 90, no. 5: 751–783.

Pettigrew, Thomas F., and Linda R. Tropp. 2008. "How Does Intergroup Contact Reduce Prejudice: Meta-analysis Test of Three Mediators." *European Journal of Social Psychology* 38, no. 6: 922-934.

Popham, R. E. 1962. "The Urban Tavern: Some Preliminary Remarks." *Addictions* 9, no. 2: 16-28.

Popham, R. E. 1978. "The Social History of the Tavern." In *Research Advances in Drug and Alcohol Problems,* edited by Y. Israel, H. Kalant, R. Popham, W. Schmidt, and R. Smart, 225-302. New York: Plenum.

Powers, Madelon. 1998. *Faces along the Bar.* Chicago: University of Chicago Press.

Radcliffe-Brown, A. R. 1940. "On Joking Relationships." *Africa* 13, no. 3: 195-210.

Rahman, Jacquelyn. 2012. "The N Word." *Journal of English Linguistics* 40, no. 2: 137-171.

Rodriguez, Nestor, and Tatcho Mindiola. 2011. "Intergroup Perceptions and Relations in Houston." In *Just Neighbors,* edited by Edward Telles, Mark Q. Sawyer, and Gaspar Rivera-Salgado. New York: Russell Sage Foundation.

Room, Robin. 1972. "Notes on Taverns and Sociability." Alcohol Research Group, Working Paper F-25, University of California, Berkeley, unpublished paper.

Rosenbaum, Thane. 2013. *Payback.* Chicago: University of Chicago Press.

Rosenfeld, Michael. 2002. "Measures of Assimilation in the Marriage Market: Mexican Americans 1970-1990." *Journal of Marriage and the Family* 64, no. 1: 152-162.

Ryder, Norman B. 1965. "The Cohort as a Concept Study of Social Change." *American Sociological Review* 30, no. 6: 843-861.

Satter, Beryl. 2009. *Family Properties: Race, Real Estate and the Exploitation of Black Urban America.* New York: Metropolitan Books.

Sheidlower, Jesse. 1999. *The F-Word.* New York: Random House.

Skalicky, Stephen, Cynthia M. Berger, and Nancy D. Bell. 2015. "The Functions of 'Just Kidding' in American English." *Journal of Pragmatics* 85 (August): 18-31.

Smedley, Audrey, and Brian D. Smedley. 2005. "Race as Biology Is Fiction, Racism as a Social Problem Is Real: Anthropological and Historical Perspectives on the Social Construction of Race." *American Psychologist* 60, no. 1: 16-26.

Spears, Richard A. 2001. *Slang and Euphemism: A Dictionary of Oaths, Curses, Insults, Ethnic Slurs, Sexual Slang and Metaphor, Drug Talk, College Lingo, and Related Matters.* 3rd and abridged ed. New York: Signet.

Spears, Richard A. 2006. *McGraw-Hill's Dictionary of American Slang and Colloquial*

Expressions. 4th ed. New York: McGraw-Hill.

Stephenson, Richard M. 1951. "Conflict and Control Functions of Humor." *American Journal of Sociology* 56, no. 6: 569-574.

Sue, Derald Wing. 2010. *Microaggressions in Everyday Life.* Hoboken, NJ: John Wiley & Sons.

Tafoya, Sonya. 2004. "Shades of Belonging." Pew Hispanic Center, Washington, DC.

Telles, Edward E., and Edward Murguia. 1990. "Phenotypic Discrimination and Income Differences among Mexican Americans." *Social Science Quarterly* 71, no. 4.

Thomas, Anthony E. 1978. "Part One: Class and Sociability among Urban Workers: A Study of the Bar as Social Club." *Medical Anthropology: Cross-Cultural Studies in Health and Illness* 2, no. 4.

Thomas, W.I. 1929. "The Child in America: Behavior Problems and Programs." *Journal of the American Medical Association* 93, no. 15: 1173.

Townsley, Eleanor. 2007. "The Social Construction of Social Facts: Using the U.S. Census to Examine Race as a Scientific and Moral Category." *Teaching Sociology* 35, no. 3: 223-238.

Uhlmann, Eric, Nilanjana Dasgupta, Angelica Elgueta, Anthony G. Greenwald, and Jane Swanson. 2002. "Subgroup Prejudice Based on Skin Color among Hispanics in the United States and Latin America." *Social Cognition* 20, no. 3: 198-225.

Vaca, Nick C. 1970. "The Mexican-American in the Social Sciences, 1912-1970, Part I: 1912-1935." *El Grito* 3 (Spring): 3-24.

Vaca, Nicolas C. 2004. *The Presumed Alliance: The Unspoken Conflict between Latinos and Blacks and What It Means for America.* New York: Harper Collins.

Valdez, Averaldo. 1997. "Intermarriage in Harris County, 1960-1990." Research Report Center for Mexican American Studies, University of Houston, Houston, Texas.

Van Maanen. 2011. *Tales of the Field.* Chicago: University of Chicago Press.

Vasquez, Jessica. 2010. *Mexican Americans across Generations: Immigrant Families, Racial Realities.* New York: New York University Press.

Vega, William Armando, Ethel Alderete, Bohdan Kolody, and Sergio Aguilar-Gaxiola. 1998. "Illicit Drug Use among Mexicans and Mexican Americans in California: The Effects of Gender and Acculturation." *Addiction* 93, no. 12: 1839-1850.

Viglione, Jill, Lance Hannon, and Roberta DeFina. 2011. "The Impact of Light Skin on Prison Time for Black Female Offenders." *The Social Science Journal*, 48, no. 1: 250-258.

Walker, Benjamin H., H. Colleen Sinclair, and John MacArthur. 2015. "Social Norms versus Social Motives: The Effects of Social Influence and Motivation to Control Prejudiced Reactions on the Expression of Prejudice." *Social Influence* 10, no. 1: 55-67.

Weaver, Charles N. 2008. "Social Distance as a Measure of Prejudice among Ethnic Groups in the United States." *Journal of Applied Social Psychology* 38, no. 3: 779-795.

Welch, Susan, and Lee Sigelman. 2011. "The 'Obama Effect' and White Racial Attitudes." *Annals of the American Academy of Political and Social Science* 634 (March): 207-220.

Wierzbicka, Anna. 1995. "Kisses, Handshakes, Bows: The Semantics of Nonverbal Communication." *Semiotica* 103, no. 3/4: 207-252.

Wilson, T.C. 1996. "Cohort and Prejudice: Whites' Attitudes Toward Blacks, Hispanics, Jews and Asians." *Public Opinion Quarterly*, 60, no. 2: 253-274.

Yancey, George. 2007. *Interracial Contact and Social Change*. Boulder, CO: Lynne Rienner Publishers.

Zenner, W.P. 1970. "Joking and Ethnic Stereotyping." *Anthropological Quarterly* 43, no. 2: 93-113.

Ziv, Avner. 2010. "The Social Function of Humor in Interpersonal Relationships." *Society* 47, no. 1: 11-18.

Index